Further Tring Personalities

by

Wendy Austin

First published October 2004
by Wendy Austin,
4 Mansion Drive,
Tring,
Hertfordshire,
HP23 5BD.

ISBN

0-9537924-2-0

Printed by Alpine Press Limited,
Station Road,
Kings Langley,
Hertfordshire.
WD4 8LF
Tel: 01923 269777

FURTHER TRING PERSONALITIES

CONTENTS

LIST OF ILLUSTRATIONS

This third and final volume of twenty Personalities from Tring and its surrounding villages contains a selection even more mixed than previously - as well as notable men and women, it includes two animals, and three ships. In fact it is curious that seven of the profiles are concerned with water in some way, which is strange in a place just about as far from the sea as it is possible to get. Perhaps it goes to show the versatility of Tring folk over the years.

Some of those featured lived their whole lives in Tring and district, while others spent little time here. Nevertheless, all contributed in some way to the shaping and history of our area.

All twenty profiles in the book are as accurate in content and detail as I have been able to establish at the time of writing. Unlike the second volume of Personalities, no fictional character is included. Although another challenge of this sort was requested by some readers, I did not wish the joke to wear too thin.

My thanks go to the very many people who have kindly supplied information, details, and reminiscences. Others have given, or lent, photographs for copying and I am indebted to Mike Bass, the British Trust for Ornithology website, the Edward Cockayne website, Leslie Emery, Jill Fowler, Violet Higginson, Harriet Jellis, Phyllis Proctor, Alan Rance, Donald Riddle, the Hon. Miriam Rothschild, The National Trust, the late Robert Timberlake, and Philip Watts.

Alec Clements has again contributed his editorial skills.

Although this is the final volume of the Tring Personalities trilogy, I am still always interested to have knowledge of any interesting local people.

W.M.A.
October 2004

ROBERT STEPHENSON 1803-1859

As the inter-city trains thunder through the great cutting at Tring, most travellers on the railway line from London to Birmingham are likely to be blissfully unaware of skill, enterprise and immense effort that made this stretch of their journey possible. It is true that the cutting does not look particularly noteworthy now, as thick vegetation clothes its sides, and it is no longer the stark scar through the chalk hillside that it was 170 years ago. The facts are that it is the longest and deepest cutting on the route; it is 2½ miles long; up to 60 feet in depth; and is as high as St Paul's Cathedral above sea level. More impressively, it took 400 men 3½ years to dig it out, using only picks and shovels, and it displaced 1,750,000 tons of spoil. This amazing feat of pre-Victorian engineering was planned and carried through by one man - Robert Stephenson.

He was born near Newcastle, and when his mother died he was two years of age. After that he was looked after by his father's sister and housekeeper. George Stephenson, a self-made man, was a tough and ambitious father, and determined that his only son would follow in his footsteps. Robert received a good education and was subjected to intensive engineering training, his father thrusting upon him the responsibility for many large projects.

George and Robert Stephenson

By 1830 the firm that George had founded was well placed to win major contracts for railway building, and he was called upon to decide which route would be most suitable for the proposed London to Birmingham railway. He delegated this decision, and the task of surveying the route, to his son. A major choice such as this which involved trading, manufacturing, and agricultural interests, was no easy job. Robert needed to tread delicately to avoid upsetting more of the gentry than necessary, which meant building the line to avoid passing near their residences or bisecting their country parks.

His first logical choice of route was through the Gade Valley, which crossed land owned, among others, by the influential Earl of Essex and the trustees of the Bridgewater estate. The map Robert produced showed the railway passing down the Gade Valley from Two Waters, through Hemel Hempstead, and onwards to Leighton Buzzard. The protests to this scheme by the local landowners were so numerous that the directors of the company asked Robert for another plan. He was forced to propose to Parliament, as his second choice, a route through the Bulbourne Valley, via Berkhamsted, and the Tring Gap. This latter involved the costly construction of a deep cutting through the chalk of the Chiltern Hills.

Even so, when his plans were published in 1831, the predictable rumpus ensued. Vigorous dissenting landowners held meetings in Berkhamsted and Watford, many of the protesters being shareholders in the existing turnpike road trust and the Grand Junction Canal Company, two concerns which would suffer great financial loss if the proposed 'iron road' was constructed. Evidence was called before the House of Lords, with Robert himself and merchants and manufacturers supporting the bill. These included William Kay (Tring Personality No.26), the owner of the silk mill. Nevertheless, the proposal was rejected, mainly due to a manoeuvre by Lord Brownlow; and the Railway Company had to think again. By the beginning of 1833 the company had reconciled many of the landowners by offering liberal compensation, which was sufficient to ensure the passage of the bill.

One objector remained disgruntled, Compte d'Harcourt of Pendley, and he demanded an exorbitant price for the land on which to site the proposed station building at Tring. Accordingly, directors of the company decided to re-position the station 3½ miles away at Pitstone Green. An account of 1840 tells us "the inhabitants of Tring were much excited on the subject .... the directors, waited on by a deputation, explained that they would willingly erect the station at the desired place, if the people of Tring would undertake to pay the difference between the price the company could afford, and that demanded by the owner". This was agreed, plus the construction of a "high road for omnibuses and coaches" from the town to the station.

Robert Stephenson was appointed engineer-in-chief for the project, his salary being £1,500 and later £2,000 a year. From that moment he devoted virtually all his time to the work. The task was large, complicated, and technically difficult, and it is said that Robert walked different stretches of the route over 30 times. Many problems had to be overcome, including the building of embankments, viaducts, awkward bridges, and two great cuttings, one of them at Tring. He had calculated that a deep cutting would be far more cost-effective than a tunnel, as longer trains could be run. However, Robert knew that one of the most complex, labour-intensive, and dangerous tasks along the whole route would be the construction of this cutting. An engineer from Smethwick secured the contract, but hopelessly under-estimated the difficulties. He was declared bankrupt, one of ten other contractors

from the original total of 30. The digging of the cutting
also exacted a heavy human price. Six workmen were
killed and countless others injured, 37 seriously. No
one, including the navvies themselves, paid much
attention to these figures; at that time it was considered
natural that death and injury accompanied such a vast
engineering undertaking.

Navvies working in Tring Cutting

Much has been written about the navvies, that race of
men, who built the cutting mostly by their own muscle.
General labourers, were recruited locally to do the digging,
but men with experience of dyke-building in the Fens of
Lincolnshire took on the main work. They lived a wild
existence, chiefly concerned with earning a few shillings a
day, usually spent on beer. The predictable result was
often violent behaviour, and towns along the route of
the railway experienced excitement seldom seen before
or since. At Tring, the navvies were housed in the
old Parsonage building, a site now occupied by the
town's library. Robert Stephenson's special gifts were
needed in the more complex matter of the organisation of

his able assistants. He was supported by five engineers, and his style of leadership inspired devotion and loyalty. The young men referred to themselves as 'Stephensonites' and remained loyal to their chief in later controversies and triumphs. A contempory pen portrait of Robert tells us he had "an energetic countenance, frank bearing, and falcon-like glance .... he was kind and considerate to his subordinates, but was not without occasional outbursts of fierce northern passion". The London to Birmingham work took its toll on him, for the account goes on "during the construction of the line, his anxiety was so great as to lead him to frequent recourse to the fatal aid of calomel" (a drug prescribed by English doctors at that time to cure practically anything).

At last the work was complete, and at the age of 34 Robert's name was made. From then on his career went from strength to strength, but was not without the problems and controversy that so often accompany feats of great engineering. After 1840 he was increasingly consulted about railways overseas, and began to travel a good deal. He also became engaged in public activity and the spread of his own business concerns. He broadened his interest further when he entered Parliament as a member for Whitby. He was a Tory of the Right - hostile to free trade, and anxious to avoid change in almost any form. This seems paradoxical in a man who was responsible for a great deal of economic and social upheaval.

A few years later Robert was again concerned with matters at Tring. He was asked by the London, Westminster & Metropolitan Water Company to advise on the feasibility of providing London with water supplies from sources in the Chiltern Hills. His reports were lengthy and, as to be expected, well-reasoned. He stated "I am well acquainted with the chalk district between Watford and Tring, and it having devolved upon me, in the course of my connexion *(sic)* with the London & Birmingham railway, to sink a great number of wells, my attention has been particularly called to the extraordinary quantity of water existing in the chalk ...." Robert's memories of work at the Tring cutting were still fresh, as he commented "The Tring cutting on the London & Birmingham Railway presents another forcible example of the constant and rapid absorption of water by the chalk. In the execution of that cutting a very large quantity of water was encountered, notwithstanding that the situation was on the summit of the chalk ridge, forming the actual brim of the basin, where it could not be supplied with any water but such as fell upon the immediate neighbourhood. The water yield is upwards of one million gallons per day, and continues to yield an extraordinary quantity up to this hour, without any sensible diminution". However, perhaps fortunately for our area, the directors of the company did not pursue the idea of using the Bulbourne Valley to supply London's water.

Tring Cutting, c.1930s

In the 1850s honours were heaped upon Robert, and all the outward marks of recognition for his distinguished career. But with his life's work completed, he became melancholy, sometimes peevish, and he often returned to visit his childhood haunts in the north-east. His constitution, never robust, finally gave way. There was never a doubt that his burial place would be Westminster Abbey, and 3,000 people packed the cathedral for his funeral service. The driver of the first engine used on the London & Birmingham line wrote to ask for a ticket - it is pleasant to record that he received one.

Sources

George and Robert Stephenson, Michael Robbins, 1966
Railways of Dacorum, The Dacorum Heritage Trust, 2000
Mr Stephenson's Second Report to
       the London Water Company, August 1841
Osborne's *London & Birmingham Railway Guide,* 1840

HARRIET JELLIS b.1923

The next two Personalities are an aunt and niece from the Franks family.

Few people are born weighing just two and a half pounds, and even fewer are born on a narrow boat. Harriet Jellis achieved both these feats and was the youngest of eight children. She survived, thanks to her mother's care, to live a robust life and herself became the mother of five children.

Harriet's parents, Ben and Emma Franks, worked the *Benjamin* and its butty (the boat in tow), which carried cargo on the Grand Union Canal between London and Birmingham. When Harriet was a toddler, the usual practice was to secure a child with rope-reins to the deck of the boat. From the early age of five, she has memories of working alongside her father, and so knew nothing of a normal childhood.

Emma Franks and her youngest son

Her parents were always busy, sometimes even through the night, and never had time to sit and talk. Harriet's education was extremely sketchy, but she and her brothers and sisters managed to teach themselves to read by puzzling out words from comics which were eagerly passed round from boat to boat. Pocket money was a half-penny a trip, and a trip could take two weeks. Harriet and her sister pooled their shares and bought a penny-worth of sticky sweets, speckled apples, or stale cakes at one of the stopping places, their favourites being Leighton Buzzard, Kings Langley, and Croxley Green.

Tragedy struck the Franks family in 1936 when Joe, Harriet's twenty-five year old brother, was drowned in a side lock at Slough. He may have been attempting to save his brother-in-law who had fallen in but, like most canal folk, neither could swim. A poignant family photograph was taken the day after the event, showing his parents, his widow, and small daughter.

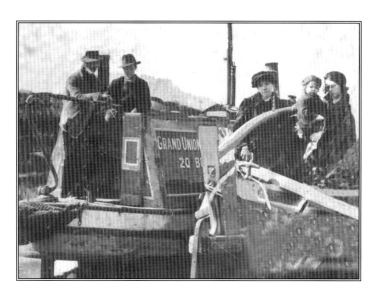

The day after Joe Franks drowned

When Harriet was 14 her parents retired from the boats and were found a house at Marsworth in *Battle Bunch*, a block of six back-to-back, one-up-one-down cottages, allocated to families who had left canal life for one reason or another. The row acquired its strange name as people used to a nomadic existence in the semi-outdoors, found conditions in these tiny cottages very restrictive, and tempers often flared and neighbours fell out. Emma Franks lived at *Battle Bunch* until the last month of her life, when she moved to be nursed at Harriet's home.

Harriet's first job was in a laundry at Berkhamsted at 6s.8d. a week, followed by wartime work at John Dickinson's helping to make paper for maps. It was hard cycling to Apsley in all weathers, and luckily Harriet had an opportunity to take a job closer to home at RMR Engineering in the old Silk Mill premises in Tring. Here the war work consisted of manufacturing parts for aircraft, and the building was painted in camouflage colours and with a gun-turret mounted on the roof. Harriet worked making detonators, later transferring to the lacquering room. She remembers it was a requirement to drink a pint of milk before going into this workroom, as apparently it was believed that this precaution nullified the effects of inhalation of fumes.

In the meantime she met her future husband playing dominoes in a local pub. William Jellis was one of 13 children from *Greystones*, three cottages opposite Startopsend Reservoir. He was a farm worker, but as Harriet and William's family increased he successfully applied for a job as lock-keeper. A tied house was provided, and they all moved to the lock house by the bridge (now tea rooms) at Lock 39, Startopsend. He was not just responsible for Lock 39 and its adjacent side locks, but for the whole flight of seven over the one-mile length of the canal at Marsworth as it descends from the Tring

Summit to the Vale of Aylesbury. Boats were not allowed through these locks at night, and the top and bottom gates of the flight were secured with a metal collar and padlock and then unlocked again each morning.

For seven years Harriet enjoyed her life at the lock house, but when William died prematurely she was left to bring up the family alone. British Waterways allowed her to remain four more years in the lock house, and she then moved to Tring, firstly to a house in Icknield Way and later to a bungalow in Faversham Close. In her retirement Harriet lives in Hemel Hempstead, her sitting room crowded with memories of an unusual life. Paintings and photographs of the canal and lock house jostle for wall space, and a glass case contains scale models of narrow boats. One of these decorated the cake on Harriet's 80th birthday, when her family arranged a day's cruise on a narrow boat, travelling the canal and passing all the local landmarks of her earlier life. Harriet confessed she spent much of that day in floods of tears.

Sources

Leighton Buzzard Observer, August 2002
Marsworth in Living Memory, Carole Fulbrook Hawkins 1998

Harriet (right), her mother and sister on the *Benjamin*

VIOLET HIGGINSON b.1932

Violet Higginson (née Franks), the niece of Harriet Jellis, was born in Hemel Hempstead, but when only a few weeks old was taken by her parents to live on their narrow boat. All her family were born into life on the canal which, despite the often large familes, could be lonely for a child. The constant travelling allowed no opportunity to make friends or play normal childish games.

It was extremely hard and Vi does not recall her childhood with any affection. Her father was employed by the carriers Fellows, Morton & Clayton of Leighton Buzzard, whose main depot was at Southall. Mr Franks was paid so much per trip at a very low rate, and if the children helped they of course were paid nothing. He was also responsible for the loading and unloading, and the cargoes comprised a variety of items including coal, sand, and timber, all of which were difficult to handle. The boat operator's duties entailed opening the lock gates, with occasional help from the lock-keeper at busy times.

Violet's parents on their wedding day

The Franks' boat was named *Kenilworth*, and the butty *Beverley*. The *Beverley* is still in use and is moored on the canal at Wolverton. It featured (in new livery) on the cover of a waterways magazine, and was once brought down to the Canal Festival at New Mill. One cabin served as living space and contained a black range, a bed, a table that pulled down, and a shelf along the back of the bed for the children. The boat was decorated by the owners, and the highly coloured water cans contained water for drinking only, and clothes had to be rinsed out in the canal. Sanitation was difficult, but Vi stressed that members of her family used a chamber pot and not a bucket, a distinction which was seemingly important. Ribbon plates, brasses and an oil-lamp decorated the inside of the cabin.

The *Beverley* at a canal festival

Schooling was spasmodic. Vi was eleven before she spent about six months at the school at Bull's Bridge, when her mother was ill before the birth of her brother. Once back on the canal, she only attended school for a few days at a time. Neither of her parents could read or write - all the paperwork was done by the staff at the carrier's yard - but Vi learned afterwards, with her husband's help. Vi's brother was a delicate little boy and most of her mother's time was spent in caring for him. His arrival meant the end of childhood for Vi, as then she was expected to help her father steer the boat and operate the locks. Like most of the children, she fell in the canal many times and had to be fished out.

Social services were also sparse. Nurse Ward (presumably paid by British Waterways) was on duty and lived at Stoke Bruerne. Sometimes a person from one of the local churches called on a Sunday. Christmas was almost always a non-event as, if the locks were open, the boats carried on working. Vi can only remember one Christmas when she had a stocking containing presents which included a longed-for doll, apple, orange and sixpence. This was when the family spent the day with her grandmother at Long Buckby. Usually the children's toys were oddments found on the towpath, and a favourite game was playing 'house' and offering tea to their friends on broken pieces of china. Vi never had any new clothes - the family's wardrobe came from a shop in a bungalow at Bull's Bridge, or a small shop at Dudswell where secondhand clothes and shoes were sold. In any case, there was no room on the boat to store clothes. Vi's mother bought groceries as needed from little premises along the way. In this area, Vi remembers shops at both *The White Lion* and *The Ship* at Marsworth.

Especially hard times occurred during the blitz when the boat happened to be in the London Docks. The family survived one of the worst air-raids of the war at Limehouse Docks, but during other raids they sometimes managed to get to the air-raid shelters. Canal boats were essential to the war effort, and carried thousands of tons of supplies. Speed was essential, and for really vital supplies packet boats could manage the round trip in five and a half days, with four or five people working a pair of boats and every lock being opened ready for the boats to go through. The winter often posed problems when the canal was iced up. Vi remembers having to stay six weeks in Leicester during one bad winter. Her father then had to sign on for the dole at the nearest local office.

Vi was pleased when parents decided in 1951 to give up the boating life and settle in Marsworth in order to help care for their dead son's children. Times were still hard as her father (due to a break of one year's service) received no pension from the carriers who employed him. He took a job as lock-keeper on the Aylesbury Arm at Marsworth. Her mother hated this period of her life; she was very lonely and any trip out meant having to cross the lock-gate outside, as no track to the house existed at that time. Her father even rode his bike across the lock-gate. Vi however loved her new life for she considered it wonderful to be able to go to the pictures and have excursions with friends. She was nearly 18 and, like her Aunt Harriet before her, obtained a job at the Silk Mill in Tring where she met her future husband. Her mother had a sad end, being in Stone Hospital for some years. Both parents are buried in Marsworth churchyard.

Vi has no nostalgia at all for the old life, remembering mostly the hardship and difficulties. She admits she has thoroughly enjoyed her time since leaving the boats with 'a lovely husband' in a house in Tring, surrounded by her personal possessions and photographs of her two daughters and grandchildren. She states she has no desire at all to have a holiday on a narrow boat, although it has been suggested to her from time to time; but says, even after over fifty years, she would have no trouble at all in navigating a boat on the Grand Union Canal from London to Birmingham.

Sources

Canal & Riverboat, October 1990
Leighton Buzzard Observer, August 2002

JOSEPH TIMBERLAKE 1874-1942
KENNETH TIMBERLAKE 1909-1972

Joseph Timberlake lived at Abbots Langley, and for a short time he worked in a local large factory at John Dickinson & Co. He then took a job at the Rothschild estate office in Tring, probably one of the most fortunate acts in his life, for the young man was talent-spotted by Lord Rothschild's agent, who asked him if he would undertake the management of the farms on the estate, approximately 5,000 acres in total. Despite Joseph's protests that he knew nothing of farming, he was persuaded to accept the job.

He soon found himself installed 800 feet above sea level at *Hastoe Farm.* Hastoe is a small hamlet a mile south of Tring, mainly clustered around the farm buildings. The climate here suited north country Dairy Shorthorn cattle, and Joseph began to specialise in this breed. He studied their genealogies carefully, and gradually the reputation of Hastoe cattle spread throughout the farming world.

Joseph Timberlake

This feat was not easy as, despite their name, cows from this breed are not consistently good milkers, and it was unusual at that time to have an animal which gave 1,000 gallons or more in a year. When this happened it was an occasion for rejoicing. (Nowadays 2,000 gallons are easily obtainable.) The old matriarch of the herd at Hastoe, named Dorothy, became a legendary figure and the ancestress of many fine bulls, which were used to upgrade the stock on neighbouring farms. The breed became particularly popular in the 1930s, and almost all cattle found in this area were Dairy Shorthorns. The cows vary in colour, sometimes a mix of brown and white, sometimes roan (known among farmers as 'red'). Shorthorns are adaptable, hardy, easily managed, and their milk yields high fat. At that time a farmer could be prosecuted if his milk production fell below the 3% standard butterfat content. As dietary opinion changed, Friesians with their high yields plus lower fat became the foremost breed.

Joseph also prided himself on his knowledge of poultry and, as well as providing for the table, his birds won many prizes under the breed name of Hastoe Cross. (The method then employed of fattening capons by force-feeding is now frowned on.)

In 1900 Joseph married and three children followed - Robert, Eunice and Kenneth, the latter following his father as manager of *Hastoe Farm*. Joseph's work kept him busy as, at that time in addition to Hastoe, he controlled seven smaller farms.

Most of the farm buildings were of solid red brick with tiled roofs, and it was Joseph's responsibility to see that all were maintained in good repair. Additionally, at Hastoe a large mill was erected, powered by a steam engine, to grind all the meal needed to feed the animals on the

Rothschild estate farms. Joseph drove himself round his new empire at a cracking pace in a light trap pulled by an elegant black pony.

The cowsheds at Hastoe comprised two wings with twenty standings in each. On a dairy farm it was of course the cowmen who were the essential workers, and the head cowman was a figure of some authority. They were a race apart from other employees, for they could get home in the middle of the day for dinner. The disadvantage was the starting time before daybreak. When the Rothschild family was in residence in their town house in London, fresh milk from both *Hastoe* and *Home Farms* was provided on their breakfast table each morning. After milking time at 4 a.m., the churns were put on a cart and driven down the steep hill to Tring Station to be loaded on the first train at dawn.

Cowmen at Hastoe, c.1904

When Lord Rothschild died in 1915, his son did not wish to farm the Hastoe estate, and Joseph was offered favourable terms to take over the tenancy of Hastoe, as well as the neighbouring farms of *Longcroft, Poors Land,* and half of Broughton pasture. He was also allowed to retain some of the best dairy stock. This led to Joseph becoming the first tenant farmer to win the Dairy Shorthorn championship at The Royal Show. Later, when Lady Rothschild died, all the estate farms were sold and, after much deliberation, Joseph took out a mortgage on his share, rightly trusting his business acumen.

As he grew older his younger son Kenneth assumed increasing responsibility for managing the farm, especially after his marriage. He became a dedicated farmer, with a love of animals, probably a legacy from his childhood when he spent many hours in the milking parlour. He continued to build up the Shorthorn herd, together with Jerseys (obtained from the *Home Farm* in Tring).
All through the pre-war years, accounts of Kenneth's success with his cows in the show ring were reported regularly in the local and national press. He joined the Shorthorn Society in 1935 and became one of the country's leading judges of pedigree cattle. Kenneth's herd grew to be nationally famous to such a degree that every farmer liked to boast that he had a bull from Mr Timberlake. He gained even more success later with Jersey cattle, and was one of very few breeders invited to judge at agricultural shows in the Channel Islands. He also served on other farming bodies, including the Milk Marketing Board.

In his spare time, Kenneth was a keen sportsman. Since his boyhood days at Berkhamsted School (when he played both rugby and cricket for the school) he had been an enthusiastic cricketer. He kept wicket for the Tring Park 1st XI, and when he was appointed captain the number of winning matches increased immediately. During the war years, despite the absence of so many players, the Cricket Club remained viable under his management. In 1948 Kenneth was delighted to accept on behalf of the club Lord Rothschild's generous gift of its ground in Station Road. (The blue and gold Rothschild colours still fly from the flagpole during home matches.) Kenneth then became one of the three trustees with responsibility of maintaining good management.

Kenneth's mother had died in 1929 at the early age of 50, and after his father's death, he gave up the splendid farm buildings at Hastoe which were unsuited to modern methods. He was content with something simpler at the top of the holloway at Hastoe - a house named *Hastoe Grove*, and a small estate of 80 acres. In 1960 he sold the major part of *Hastoe Farm* and the adjoining *Longcroft Farm* for a total of £37,500; the auction was held at the *Rose & Crown Hotel*, the purchaser being L E Allen of St.Leonards. In the same year Kenneth's famous herd of Shorthorn cattle were sold, including many champions of both the Royal and London Dairy Shows.

Probably Kenneth Timberlake never intended to retire completely from his life in farming. In any case he did not have the chance to enjoy any leisure in old age because he and his wife were involved in a bad car accident on Pendley Hill which left her confined to a wheelchair. A little later Kenneth died suddenly and prematurely when he collapsed whilst driving cattle in Hastoe Row.

The year after Kenneth's death both his house and 80 acres of farmland were put up for sale by auction at the *Rose & Crown* at Tring. Broken into five lots which realised a total of £115,900, the particulars stated "a delightful small estate in the beautiful Chilterns".

MAKE THIS A DATE

23rd May 1960

when the

HASTOE HERD

world-famous for good udders and beautiful type of cattle,
achieved by line breeding since 1898, will be dispersed at

HASTOE FARM · TRING

1898-1915 Tring Park   1915-1960

Barrington Duchess 31st
(Geo. Taylor)

Hastoe Barrington Duchess 22nd
(A 2,500 gallon cow)

Many of this family will be for sale and some past and future show winners,
Proven Stock Bulls **and the son of Waveney Veracity 2nd**

Championships and Reserve Championships at the Royal and London
Dairy Shows won by Hastoe cows and cows by Hastoe bulls include :

Royal
1935	Hastoe Millicent 2nd
1936	Kelmscott Marjorie 47th
1937	Hastoe Barrington 17th
1949	Wild Queen 20th
1950	Wild Queen 20th
1957	Waveney Veracity 2nd
1931	Hastoe Charming Lass
1932	Hastoe Wild Queen 11th
1951	Hastoe Lady Hermione
	45th
1957	Headlands Lady Lucy

London Dairy Show
1933	Hastoe Beauty 7th
1949	Hastoe Lady Hermione
	45th
1950	Hastoe Barrington 3rd
1956	Hastoe Winsome
1959	Waveney Veracity 2nd

The Hastoe herd has won the Calvert Cup three times
Waveney Veracity 2nd created a record by winning
Championship at the Royal and London Dairy Shows

Sale by Messrs. John Thornton and Co. for J. TIMBERLAKE and SON. *Tring 3342*
Herd can be seen any time by appointment

The disposal of the Hastoe herd

During the Rothschild era, up to a dozen men had been employed by the Timberlakes, but at the time of Kenneth's death he was managing his smaller acreage with just one man to help him. Local people watched sadly as Hastoe farmhouse and its associated dairy buildings, rick-yard, and mill gradually fell into disrepair, and no longer echoed with the comforting farmyard sounds of lowing cows and clanking milk pails. Although no longer a farm, the complex had a new beginning in the 1990s, when its forlorn aspect changed completely as all the buildings were restored and converted into attractive private dwellings.

Sources

The Bucks Herald archives

Hertfordshire's Past 39, Hastoe near Tring, R R Timberlake 1995

Tring Park Cricket Club Sesquicentennial 1836-1986, David Kempster

Seventy Summers, Tony Harman 1986

LIONEL MARTIN 1878 - 1945

During the infancy of motor sports from 1904 onwards, Aston Hill near Tring was the Mecca of all motorcycle and racing car enthusiasts. The long steep twisting gradient provided a stimulating challenge for those who wished to test both their machines and their driving skills, against each other. On a day in April 1914, in clouds of dust and to enthusiastic cheers, Lionel Martin in a modified 10hp Singer car roared up Aston Hill to claim first place on this acknowledged difficult hill-climb. He became so fond of this motoring venue that when he registered his first sporting light car less than a year afterwards, he named it Aston-Martin (the hyphen has since been dropped). Now a stone-built cairn at the top of the hill commemorates his achievement, and bears a plaque inscribed "the start of a legend in the history of the automobile".

Participation in the sport of motor racing is not cheap, and Lionel was fortunate in being born into a family who owed their fortune to the English china clay mines in Cornwall. His expensive education at Eton, and later at a small private college in Oxford helped him to establish contacts in the social circles to which he turned later to help finance his automobile enterprises.

Lionel Martin

Whilst at Oxford he became interested in cycle racing, and competed successfully in both bicycle and tricycle races and trials. It was a natural progression from this sport to motor racing, and before long Lionel bought his first automobile. His love of speed quickly became apparent when he came into conflict with the Richmond justices who fined him £20 with 9 guineas costs, and the Guildford Bench a further fine of £10 with £6.10s.6d. costs.   His driving licence was suspended for two years, and Lionel was said to have grown fat and, in consequence, to have resumed his cycling activities. It was at this time that he met Robert Bamford, and in 1912 the two men established a partnership running a motor business off Fulham Road. That same year Lionel visited the automobile show at Olympia and purchased a 10hp Singer car at the show stand. He modified its engine to such good effort that this undistinguished little car attained a speed of 70 mph while still remaining completely reliable. In this same car two years later Lionel achieved his memorable success on Aston Hill.

A year previously, tragedy had struck when his young wife, Christine, died shortly after the birth of their son. Lionel re-married after the first war, and his bride Katherine, a vivacious and impulsive girl, entered whole-heartedly into his motoring activities. A skilled and daring driver in her own right, she accompanied her husband on many of his trips with prototype cars, often taking the wheel on difficult hill-climbs. Throughout the time of Lionel's involvement with Aston Martin cars, Katherine continue to played a vital, but sometimes diastrous, role.

All who knew Lionel Martin agreed that his manners were those of a perfect gentlemen. He was well liked and is remembered as "a genial and bustling individual, very proud of the old school, and modest about his successes with the Singer at Aston Clinton and elsewhere". He was generous in his help to others, hospitable, and he loved good food, good wine, and good living. He and Katherine kept 'open house' at their homes, first in Kensington, and then at Kingston-on-Thames: all who called were welcomed warmly, and invited to stay and enjoy Katherine's excellent cooking.

Lionel and Robert began to experiment with building 'specials', the best consisting of a 1389 cc. Coventry-Simplex engine on the chassis of a 1908 Isotta-Fraschini racing voiturette. When it was complete, the vehicle was entered for several trials, but the outbreak of World War I saw a stop on all sporting activities. The partners closed shop and sold all their equipment to the Sopwith Aviation Company. During the conflict Lionel worked for the Admiralty and continued to use his car throughout the war. It was not until 1918 that they were able to relaunch the business, and with a capital of £1,000 they acquired an agency for Singer cars in Henniker Place, Kensington. The agency also sold and serviced Calthorpe and GWK cars. Building 'specials' continued but, possibly due to shortage of supplies, Lionel and Robert were able to make no more than four before 1921. That same year saw the first car to carry the Aston Martin name ready for the road.

Whether the two men disagreed is not known, but for whatever reason Robert Bamford wished to dissolve the partnership, and his shares in the firm were bought by Lionel's wife. The business relocated to Abingdon Road, South Kensington, described as "unassuming little premises next door to a United Dairies Milk Depot". Here several racing cars with twin-ohc engines were built; these were well received and led Lionel to announce that he intended to build 100 cars over a three-year period. Production began in 1922 with a light sports car of simple design. (For the technically minded it had a ladder-type steel frame with channel-section side members, and carried

both axles on parallel semi-elliptic leaf-springs. The
4-cylinder L-head 1496 cc. engine had a three-bearing
crankshaft, Zephyr iron pistons, and steel connecting rods,
drilled for lightness.)

The bulk of the money for his enterprise was roughly
equivalent to at least two to three million pounds in
today's terms, and came mainly from Lionel himself. He
also gained backing from the colourful racing driver, Count
Louis Vorow Zborowski, who put up £10,000 and drove
the cars. The Count was particular in his racing demands,
and when he wanted a competitive car he arranged to
have a colleague draw up a 4-cylinder derivative of the
Ballot Grand Prix straight-8 for Aston Martin. At least two
of these engines were made by Rover and mounted in a
special Aston Martin chassis.

The marque became well known and admired in racing
circles, but few customers bought Lionel's cars. In less
than two years it became apparent that even the massive
sum he had supplied was proving insufficient for the
costly business of constructing racing cars. It was
necessary to relaunch the company and Lionel called upon
an enthusiastic friend, and old Etonian, the Honorable
John Benson, who persuaded his mother, Lady
Charnwood, to provide a large sum. Even this did not
solve the company's problems and, after making some 69
cars, on each of which money was lost, Bamford & Martin
(as it was still called) went into receivership.

This lowest point in the fortunes of the firm triggered a
period of acrimony and legal actions. John Benson,
understandably upset over the loss of money and prestige,
made disparaging remarks about the Martins, who duly
sued for damages for alleged slander. Both parties
engaged top KCs, and the sorry outcome was a verdict in
favour of the plaintiff (Lionel), but with an award of a

paltry one penny and three farthings in damages. What emerged then, and later, was that although Lionel was liked and admired by most people, the strong-minded Katherine was regarded as rather bossy and vindictive. She was feared by the personnel in the works, and friends and acquaintances nicknamed her "Calamity Kate".

Lionel left the works for the last time on 13th November 1925 and played no part in the subsequent history of Aston Martin. He concentrated on his mining interests, but the famous name remained. Lionel was known to be a perfectionist, and it may be that his expectations for his cars were simply too high. A loyal customer of the time remembered "Aston Martins were in every way excellent cars with refinement, good road-holding, good brakes, good lines, and respectable performance from the 35 bhp one-and-a-half-litre side-valve engine. They were also extremely expensive". When the firm was reorganised it was known as Aston Martin Motors Ltd, capitalised at £14,000, and established in the former Citroen assembly plant at Hanworth Air Park. The rest, as they say, is history.

Lionel Martin weathered the bitter disappointment at the failure of his project, but for the rest of his life maintained an interest in the sport of motor racing. He was a member of the RAC Competitions Committee, and seldom missed a major Brooklands meeting, where he acted as a steward or marshal. Illness afflicted his last years but indomitable as ever, he took up the passion of his youth of riding racing tricycles. This made his wife nervous, and with good reason when an accident in 1944 left him with broken thigh bones. He told visitors to the hospital "I'll get on my trike once I'm invalided home!". Sadly for Katherine, Lionel carried out his threat, was knocked from his machine at traffic lights in Kingston, and died one week later.

Lionel Martin on the Aston Hill Climb

In September 2003 a classic Aston Martin car made history again on a stretch of road between Tring and Aston Clinton. When the Transport Minister, Tony McNulty, opened the new four-mile £25m. extension of the A41 by-pass, the car in which he was driven was chosen to echo the earlier motoring achievement on Aston Hill. After years of petitioning and waiting, the village was able to celebrate and watch the V8 Vantage Aston Martin break the blue ribbon, and drive down the road that had taken three years to build.

Sources

The Beaulieu Encyclopædia of the Automobile, Vol.1, 2000
'Aston Martin leaves its marque', David Burgess-Wise
Lionel Martin, a biography, A B Demaus 1980
The Berkhamsted Gazette, 8 October 2003

The Origin of Aston Martin

From 1904 to 1925,
Aston Hill, part of the Lord Rothschild's Estate,
was a renowned motoring venue.

Lionel Martin made his first ascent of this hill,
in a tuned Singer car, on the 4th. April, 1914.
Shortly afterwards, on the 16th. May, at the
Herts County Automobile and Aero Club meeting,
he was so successful, that the sporting light car
first registered in his name in March 1915,
was called an "ASTON-MARTIN".

It was the start of a legend
in the history of the automobile.

This plaque was placed here
by the Aston Martin Owners Club
and
Aston Martin Lagonda Limited.

The plaque on the monument at Aston Hill

JAMES STEVENS 1808 - 1911

Despite the wonders of modern medicine, it is true that reaching the age of 100 years is considered an achievement worthy of comment. A hundred years ago this feat was truly remarkable and, as the person concerned progressed through his or her late nineties towards the magic figure, fame was assured by constant references and health bulletins in the local news.

As a humble farm labourer, James Stevens never expected much attention to be shown to him but, by the time he died in 1911 at the age of 103, his was a household name in Tring and district. Known to all as 'Grampy Stevens', for many years after his death his portrait in oils hung in the Church House. Although he would have known nothing of the science of genetics, he may always have been aware that he could reach a great age because his grandmother died at 104, and his mother at 101; and they lie respectively in Hulcott and Long Marston churchyards.

Born at Astrope, James could boast that he had lived during the reign of six monarchs. He was baptised at Puttenham, and used to relate that he narrowly escaped death by an accidental scalding he received on the very day of his christening. Until the age of 75 he worked as a labourer on the land, serving a variety of employers on different farms in an area from Hastoe to Drayton Beauchamp; for the last fifteen years of his working life he was employed by Mr Dawe of *Home Farm*, Tring. This was before the Rothschilds acquired the Tring Park estate, and for a time he also served the Reverend James Williams who lived at the mansion in the Park.

James could have stepped out of the pages of a Thomas Hardy novel, for he never abandoned the standard smock of early Victorian agricultural labourers. This embroidered garment was woven in Tring in the canvas weaving shop in Park Road. It may be that he cultivated this quaint image, and his picturesque appearance drew loud comments in the street on his first visit to London.

In 1908 when James reached 100, a big fuss was made and his picture appeared in 'The Farmer and Stockbreeder' magazine, a recognition that the farming world felt he had earned. By then, it had been appreciated how a farm labourer in the previous century must have struggled to support a large family. In common with thousands of others, James lived through several severe agricultural depressions, when work was scarce and hours unbelievably long. He used to recount that his regular wage was eight shillings a week, from which he managed to save five pounds by the age of 26, when he married his wife at Drayton Beauchamp church. The marriage produced 13 children and, at the time of his death, James left 52 direct descendants. After 44 years of married life, his wife died, leaving him a widower for 33 years. For some time he lived alone at No.8 Henry Street, Tring, and later moved to be with his daughter and family.

James Stevens in 1908

James took all that life offered, good or ill, with a calm philosophy, supported by his religious faith. The great industrial advances of the Victorian age left him somewhat bemused, but he remembered clearly the advent of the railway and, late in life, consented to ride in a train. Although he never had the opportunity to travel in a motor car, he viewed these with great interest. However he could not be persuaded to believe that aeroplanes had any future.

In his late nineties, James survived several minor accidents, including a bad fall in Frogmore Street. He was rescued by the local police constable and taken to a nearby shop: the resourceful officer borrowed a wheelchair from the vicarage and pushed him home. A few years later, James' end came peacefully when he died in his sleep at his daughter's house.

Local people considered that he should be remembered, and the vicar volunteered to receive any donations towards a suitable memorial. A plain cross of Hollington red stone prepared by masons in Tring was placed at the head of James' grave in the beautiful churchyard at Drayton Beauchamp, where he lies next to his wife. James Stevens would probably be amazed to know that he is still remembered in Tring, and that his photograph has appeared in several historical records of the town.

Sources

The Bucks Herald archives
Tring Parish Magazine, March 1911

In medieval times Pendley Manor was owned by the Whittingham family, but after the demise of the third Sir Robert (Tring Personality No.6), his daughter Margaret and her husband, John Verney, inherited the estate, and for one hundred years, four generations of the Verney family lived at the house. They are remembered by a fine brass in Aldbury Church.

In 1553 Margaret and John's great-grandson, Edmund, fell into disfavour with Mary Tudor - not a difficult thing to do - and was ordered to keep to his house during the queen's pleasure. He had no children, and the manor passed to his nephew, Francis, then a minor. This Verney is the most interesting of the whole family, as dissolute and dashing figures always capture the imagination more than their worthy relatives. Pendley seems an unlikely cradle for a soldier of fortune or a buccaneer, but Francis Verney took up both careers.

According to the Verney papers of 1853, the seeds of his "wild and unhappy life" probably started at the age of five when he lost his mother. Further damage was caused when his father remarried, and his new wife persuaded her husband to divide the Verney inheritance between Francis and her own son, requiring ratification by Act of Parliament. She added to the problems by arranging a childhood wedding between fourteen-year-old Francis, and Ursula, her own young daughter by a previous marriage. These two actions gave her an interest in both halves of the Pendley estate, as well as the Manors of Quainton and Fleet Marston.

The Bursar's accounts at Trinity College, Oxford, show that Francis matriculated in 1600, aged fifteen. The next year his father died and was interred at Aldbury, and then Francis is known as living at St Dunstan's-in-the-West in London, where one of his servants was killed - it was thought during a drunken brawl. A year later Francis attained his majority, and still smarting over the loss of what he considered his rightful inheritance he lost no time in quarrelling with his step-mother. He contested the decision of Parliament vigorously, and brought an action to reverse the previous ruling. After a lengthy legal struggle a new bill was drafted, but following "much dispute and argument" it was rejected.

Writhing under a sense of presumed injustice Francis, now overwhelmed with debt, determined to sell everything, and free himself from the pressure of creditors. His alarmed step-mother made only one concession, granting him the Manor of Quainton. This was was too little, and too late, for Francis was set on his course, and vowed to forsake his country and the friends who he thought had injured him. His married state did not keep him at home, for the union with Ursula was not one made in heaven. She was bad-tempered and shrewish, although Francis may have contributed by his behaviour. A handsome and reckless young man, with a deep hatred of his step-mother (who also happens to be his wife's mother) is unlikely to be good husband material.

Quainton and its 800 acres was sold first, for only £500, and Fleet Marston went next. Francis was further resolved to dispose of the family's ancient mansion of Pendley, together with Bunstrux Manor in Tring, and ensured the break-up of the whole house and home by selling the lands, residences, and even the furniture to the new owner.

The Verney family reeled under the impact of Francis's vindictive actions, for of course there was no way in which they could remain at the family seat. No alternative offered itself but removal to the depths of rural Buckinghamshire, to re-establish themselves in another of their country houses.

Pendley Manor, c. 1630

Having disposed of everything that was saleable, he gave an irrevocable authority to one of his uncles to act for him in all business connected with the wreck of the Verney estate, and assigned all his title deeds to a second uncle. He then disappeared to the Holy Land. His activities over the next few years are not well documented, but one report stated "this Francis was a great traveller and fought several Duellos". He appears to have thrown in his lot with a band of English volunteers under the command of Captain John Giffard, a member of the family who had leased another of the Verney estates at Middle Claydon in Buckinghamshire.

Meanwhile Francis was attracted by Giffard's adventurous plan to support Muley Sidan's claim to the throne of Morocco. Such a war was of no interest to the English, but the barbarity, liberal pay, and exotic location undoubtedly held fascination for Francis, and like-minded young men. Muley Sidan numbered among his supporters 200 Englishmen who volunteered for this singular service.

It is recorded that Sidan bestowed on Giffard "a rich sword, valued at a thousand marks, and a scarlet cloake richly embroidered with pearle, sent as a present from the late sovereigne of famous memory queene Elizabeth". Early in the war Muley Sidan sent for his wizards and soothsayers to foretell the success of the fight. They answered that he would regain the throne later, but would lose the imminent battle. On hearing this dire prophesy, Sidan desperately tried to withdraw his troops, but some were cut to pieces, and others resorted to shameful flight. He urged his English supporters to be gone, and gave Giffard a good horse, but the English forces were of sterner stuff and retorted "they had not come thither to run, but rather to die an honourable death". Die many of them did, but not Francis.

Sir Francis Verney

After this escapade, he joined the vessel *Fortune* under the command of Giffard's nephew, Richard, and he then engaged in a career of piracy on the high seas. During the reign of Elizabeth I the national hatred of the Spanish, and envy of their commerce, led a great number of English privateers to chance their luck in plundering foreign ships for booty. (Throughout the sixteenth century the career of buccaneer was not considered a disgraceful occupation, and both the queen and general populace encouraged such activity.)

However, not all English pirates confined their looting to Spanish ships. Sometimes they turned on their own countrymen, and in 1609 the embassy in Spain sent word home that "Verney had taken three or four Poole shipps and one of Plymouth". Understandably, James I closed English ports to the privateers, and they were forced to seek other harbours in which to refit their vessels. They then based their activities on Tunis, Algiers, and other towns on the Barbary coast, where everyone who robbed Christians was made most welcome.

The wild career of Francis continued for a few more years, and one account records that he was captured by Sicilians, and served as a galley slave. True or not, it is certain that a life so reckless could not last long. In 1615 he was dropped by a passing ship at the Hospital of St Mary of Pity at Messina, and there he died in poverty. Where he is buried is not known. A certificate of his decease was brought home by an English merchant, together with a turban, two silk pelisses, and two pairs of Turkish slippers. This pathetic little collection included his pilgrim's staff which implies that, although he may have adopted native dress, he retained the religion which some thought he had rejected by 'turning Turk'.

In 1606 after the mayhem caused by Francis, the Verney

family departed Pendley for ever, to live on their other estate in Buckinghamshire. Claydon House is now the property of The National Trust, and among its treasures are a few mementoes of Sir Francis Verney, as well as his full-length portrait. This shows an aristocratic young man, with Vandyke beard, dressed in the very height of Jacobean fashion, gazing confidently at the viewer. It offers no hint of his dissipation and the unconventional life that followed.

Sources

The Verneys of Claydon, Sir Harry Verney, 1968

The Verney Papers, 1853

Historical discourse of Muley Hamet's rising, 1619

73.1911.encyclopædia.org

'Aldbury's three mansions (3)', Jean Davis

The Battle of Trafalgar on the 21st October 1805 was the decisive sea battle of the Napoleonic war, fought in the vicinity of the south-west coast of Spain.

An essential feature in Napoleon's plan for the invasion of Britain was the control of the Channel area whilst his armies were crossing. In an attempt to achieve this, the French fleets at Toulon and Brest were ordered to evade the blockading British squadrons by sailing to the West Indies and then doubling back, having drawn the main British fleet across the Atlantic. A game of cat and mouse ensued between Lord Nelson and the French admiral, Villeneuve. Nelson gave chase and followed the French to Cadiz, their objective to capture Gilbraltar. At daybreak on the 21st of October the two fleets were about 11 miles apart, and Nelson signalled to form the order of sailing into two columns, and to prepare for battle. His plan was to crush part of the enemy fleet before it could be relieved by the remainder, and Nelson himself was to lead the line which would cut through the centre of the enemy's strength. At 12.20 p.m. *Victory,* flying the signal "Engage the Enemy" fired her first broadside.

The *Victory*

The glories and tragedies that followed are now history, recorded in statues, paintings, films, and books. An enormous amount has been written, and is still being written, about Lord Nelson, his captains and other officers, but very little about the ordinary members of the crew. Most were illiterate, and in any case the habit of letter-writing was almost unknown among seamen who had little to write about, as their usual duties entailed tedious months, or even years, of patrolling the Channel, and blockading Napoleon's sea-ports.

However, we know that one of these ordinary men, Henry Harding, came from Tring, Hertfordshire, as his name and home town are recorded on the Muster Roll of the crew of Victory. Other facts that we can be sure about are that he was aged 32 at the time of the battle; his enlistment date as a Private in the Royal Marines was 17th April 1803; his muster number was M.47 in Chatham Company 85; and after the wars he was awarded the Naval General Service medal.

Henry may have joined the Marines after seeing a poster placed by one of the Recruiting Sergeants who were known to visit market towns such as Tring, (or he may even have taken the King's Shilling accidently when the sergeant surreptitiously slipped it into Henry's tankard of ale). The inducements to join the service included tales of adventure and excitement in foreign lands, the promise of free food and accommodation whilst on board ship, and a bounty of £26. The war against France had led to this generous offer, but many a young man lived to regret enlisting as it meant a period of indefinite service. Henry also received a Brown Bess (flintlock) musket, a smart uniform whose design had recently been approved by the King, a black hat with a cockade, and a pair of boots. After leaving his home he was subjected to intensive training at Chatham, and received £1.18s.0d. a week on land, and 19s.3d whilst at sea.

A Royal Marine contingent joined *Victory* when she was being fitted out, and once on board Henry's life was not likely to be particularly pleasant. Long periods of boredom, interspersed with terrifying bloody action, when mutilation or death were a distinct possibility, was the lot of all those who sailed with the Navy in the time of Nelson. Much of Henry's time was spent on the lower gun deck, separated from the seamen, in conditions which were dank, rat-infested, and dark as a dungeon. Meals were taken on mess-tables slung from the beams, and the diet comprised dried meat, hardtack (weevil-infested ship's biscuit), and water stored for many months in wooden casks, often green and full of living organisms. Along with the other 170 marines, he would have been accustomed to a total lack of privacy, for his sleeping hammock was slung between the guns and only fourteen inches away from his fellows on either side. His personal possessions were likely to be few, and in any case liable to be stolen. Almost the only lawful pleasure permitted was the daily rum ration.

At that time soldiers and ordinary seamen regarded marines as fitting into neither profession, so Henry and his comrades were accorded low social status and regarded with scorn. Their duties at sea did not help their popularity, as one of their main tasks was sentry duty, and standing guard on deck whilst the brutal punishments were being meted out. They were also needed to insure the ship against mutiny whilst afloat, and desertion whilst in port. During a sea battle, some marines would be ordered to shed their scarlet tunics, stow their weapons, and help a gun crew in the running out, preparation, priming, loading, and firing one of the 100 guns carried by Victory. Others were lined up along the rails with muskets at the ready to repel boarders; long steel-tipped boarding pikes and sharpened cutlasses were placed amidships ready for use by marine parties boarding the enemy's ships.

Shortly after dawn on the morning of 21st October 1805 the decks of *Victory* were cleared for action. The ship's company took their breakfast, and were ordered to quarters in readiness for Nelson's inspection. Adored by both his officers and men, his words of encouragement and optimism heartened the whole crew as he toured the ship. After that Henry and his friends had plenty of time to contemplate what lay ahead, as it was some hours before the two fleets slowly drew close enough to engage. In every ship tension and excitement mounted until, finally, the most famous battle signal ever sent - "England expects every man to do his duty" - was hoisted to the masthead of *Victory*, soon to be followed by crashing broadsides from the enemy's guns.

The deck of *Victory* with Nelson and Marines

Late in the afternoon when it was all over, fatigue, anti-climax, and grief over the death of Nelson and other shipmates, affected the crew, and there was little rejoicing at the tremendous victory in which they had participated. As the ship's wheel had been smashed, *Victory* was taken into tow, and after several days of storms, she limped into the safe haven of Gibraltar.

Years later, survivors probably told and re-told their story to comrades in arms, and to family and friends, and were rightly regarded as heroes. It is a pity that we do not know if Henry Harding ever came home to Tring to tell his tale first hand.

One local Royal Marine who did return after Trafalgar was David Newton who fought on the *Revenge*: he was wounded in the battle and received recompense. He was completely blind in old age, and lived with his son at Cholesbury. It was not until the minister of the church petitioned on his behalf for a pension that David was awarded 10s.6d. a week until his death at the age of 99. (His grave can be seen in Cholesbury churchyard.)

After Trafalgar only the flag-officers and captains who fought on that day received decorations, with the issue of a gold medal and clasp authorised by the King. In the years of peace after the wars, it was realised how much there was to commemorate, but it was not until 1841 that Queen Victoria approved the award of a naval medal for all the officers and men who took part in the battles of the Napoleonic wars. In 1847 she personally presented silver medals to all seamen who fought in these actions, but few were still alive to receive them from her hands. It would be nice to think that Henry Harding was among the white-haired and weather-beaten veterans who were honoured in this way. This fact will never be known, but we can be certain that a Tring man was present on

Victory, and contributed to that turning point in British history.

Sources

www.hms-victory.com
Trafalgar, The Nelson Touch, David Howarth 1969
Nelson's War, Peter Padfield 1976
Encyclopædia Britannica

MARIE JACK O.B.E. 1915 - 2002

In 1919 Grace Cone founded a School of Dancing, and three years later another artistic lady, Olive Ripman, established a similar institution. The year 1947 saw the amalgamation of these two ventures, based at Stratford Place in west London. This was no ordinary school, as its founders believed that a talent for the performing arts should be encouraged by the expedient of rigorous training.

The enterprise flourished to such an extent that it was apparent that additional premises were needed, and a suitable building for a second school was found in the countryside at the old Rothschild mansion in Tring Park. At that time it was known as the Cone-Ripman School, and an advertisement was placed in The Bucks Herald newspaper announcing its arrival and adding that "The drive and grounds surrounding the mansion are therefore private property for use of the school only. The principal would be grateful if the residents of Tring would kindly respect this notification".

The following year a minor dispute arose when an outbreak of diphtheria at the school necessitated an application for beds at the local Isolation Hospital on the road to Little Tring. The Council considered the matter and decided that private schools should be asked to pay for the treatment of their pupils, and accordingly requested 12s. a day per child. Eventually a compromise was reached, and it was settled that the school should find a sum of around £2 a week.

These local difficulties between the school and Tring were largely resolved when a fire started in a common room at three o'clock in the morning, and the town fire brigade arrived within five minutes. The brigade's action was greatly praised, and then Tring and the school began to live happily together. By 1949 the Cone-Ripman pupils (all girls) were entertaining townsfolk with a display of dancing in the Victoria Hall. The children became a familar sight on Sundays, with their white gloves and boaters, filing down to the Parish Church for morning service. Their general tidiness and perfect manners were held up as an example by mothers of Tring's own children.

In the post-war years the ethics of courtesy, tidiness, and discipline were strongly upheld by the Principals of the Arts Educational School (as it became), and especially by Mrs Marie Jack. She joined the teaching staff at the London school in the early 1950s, taking classes in English and Geography. Her skills as a leader and administrator were such that, within a few years, she was appointed Principal. Changes at the Arts Educational School came in 1966 when the four founding directors retired, and the directorship of the Trust was taken by the well-known ballerina, Beryl Grey.

More reorganisation occurred two years later when Marie Jack was invited to assume responsibility for both the London and Tring schools. In the 21 years since its founding, the school at Tring had grown from a total of 45 to 245 pupils, and it was therefore a compliment to Marie's talents that she was appointed to undertake both tasks.

Mary Isabella Davies, always known as Marie, was born in Australia where her father worked in the mining industry. At the age of five she returned with her family to Wales where she was educated at Pontywaun Grammar School, Gwent, and at the University of Wales in Cardiff. Marie was a born teacher, for she had an uncanny understanding of what went on in children's minds. On first meeting, her imposing presence and deep voice made her seem formidable, both to children and to their parents. This impression was soon dispelled as, although strict and not prodigal with praise, she was always fair, and it was probably this latter quality and her sense of humour, that earned respect from her pupils and staff.

Marie Jack

Marie's commitment to the school was total, and she was seldom off duty for she occupied a private flat within the mansion. She never let her girls be in doubt that the very highest standard was always expected. On one occasion, after a pupil had performed an exceptionally brillant 'cello rendition, her class-mates broke into spontaneous applause. Marie stamped her foot and ordered them to stop, explaining that it was only what was expected. Her methods produced results, and it was during her years of headship that the schoool won Sainbury's prestigious Choir of the Year award, the finals being held in Buxton.

The one thing that is always still remembered when Marie Jack's name is mentioned is her insistence that her schoolgirls should curtsey to the teachers and adult visitors. Until her retirement, this quaint old-fashioned custom was retained at the school, even though the world had long since moved on.

She relinquished the headship of the London School in 1986, but remained at Tring for three more years. Her husband, Thomas, a doctor, had died earlier and on her retirement Marie settled in Bath, finally moving to a residential home in London.

The school has built on the early foundations imposed by Marie and other principals. Boys are now included, and the pupils from the age of eight to 18 all have an interest in, and a talent for, the performing arts. Now 275 children study dance, drama, and music, and simultaneously pursue normal academic studies. The school is still sometimes referred to as 'the ballet school' by older Tring residents, and it is true that classical ballet remains the foundation of the Dance course, but other types of dance are taught to encourage a high level of technical skill and aesthetic awareness.

The Tring Park mansion was often the scene of the Rothschild family's lavish entertainment of Royalty and all the great and the good of late-Victorian and Edwardian society. But the main reception rooms are now empty of all furnishings, and they echo with the sound of practice pianos. In his Lordship's smoking room, high above the chimney-piece, the scantily-clad marble statue of *Victory* still perches gracefully on the toes of one foot, but no longer overhears weighty discussions on matters of state. She now gazes down on the pupils performing ballet, contemporary, and tap-dance routines. In the school's modern theatre, public performances of music, drama, and dance have become an established feature of Tring town life.

If Marie Jack was still alive, she would be proud of the work carried out by 'her' school, although most likely she would express her astonishment at the modern fashions worn by the pupils. One highlight of her career was a visit to the school by the Duchess of Kent in the 1970s, and she would have been delighted by two recent landmarks when some pupils performed with the National Youth Ballet at *Sadlers' Wells*, and the Chamber Choir were invited to appear before the Prince of Wales at Stoke Mandeville.

Sources

The Daily Telegraph, 20 July 2002
The Bucks Herald archives

CHARLES SEABROOK 1865 - 1948

In the nineteenth century young working-class boys were no strangers to a hard life. Charles Seabrook, born before school attendance was compulsory, never had any formal education, and worked from about the age of 11 until he was pensioned at 72. He did not achieve fame, local or otherwise, but the story of his life can be thought to illustrate all that is best in the late Victorian age. Very early on he realised he would achieve nothing unless he taught himself reading, writing and arithmetic, and this self-help stood him in good stead as he began to be held in high regard by his employers, and when he needed to provide a secure and happy home for his large family.

Charles married Lucy Busby in 1889, and his job as a stableman and groom on the Tring Park estate entitled him to live in a Rothschild lodge house in Park Road. In those far-off days, nightingales nested in the woods along that road, and after dark Charles used to take Lucy to hear them sing.

Charles and Lucy Seabrook

Later the couple moved to another Rothschild-owned house at No.88 Western Road, which had an unusual advantage. An enormous bath along one wall of the kitchen, together with facilities in an outbuilding at the rear of the house, enabled Lucy to earn extra income by washing, starching, and ironing items of clothing from the Tring Park house.

This welcome addition to the budget allowed the large family of seven children to enjoy more pastimes, such as music lessons. Charles is remembered as a good father who, unusually in those days, never used corporal punishment. On just one memorable occasion he raised his hand to son Billy, who without asking had borrowed his father's leather working gauntlets to play snow-balls. Billy returned with soaking wet gloves, and had the bright idea of drying them in the oven of the kitchen range before his father came home. Predictably, the leather crinkled and cracked, and Billy got a sound smacking.

Charles loved animals, and it may be that this led to his promotion as kennel man assuming responsibility for the Rothschild hounds and the family's pet dogs. In those pre-quarantine days, owners had freedom to take their animals abroad when they wished, and Charles was required to travel with the dogs when the Rothschilds wanted their pets to accompany them.

The Rothschild family at Tring were very fond of dogs, and group photographs often include their pets. Lord Rothschild can be seen posing with *Snip*, his own small dog who followed him everywhere and accompanied him on his carriage drives. *Snip*, along with all the other family pets, was buried in the dogs' cemetery on the edge of the Park, and it is likely that this sad task was included among Charles' duties.

Charles with Pomeranians

Another important part of his work was the care and exercise of the prize-winning Pomeranians owned by Richardson Carr, the Agent of the Tring Park estate. These little dogs were kennelled at the *Home Farm* in Park Road, and their long fluffy coats required constant cleaning and grooming. When the Poms were exhibited at dog shows on the Continent, Charles went with them. Puppies from champion bitches were sold, and once when Charles was particularly busy, he entrusted his daughter, Bertha, with the task of carrying a puppy in a basket two miles to Tring Station. She was a soft-hearted child, felt sorry for the little chap, and en route thought it would be kind to let him have a run. It evaded capture for quite a while, and when Bertha finally caught it the dog was so dirty, she decided to go home and confess. It was hurriedly cleaned and brushed in time to catch a later train.

Strict punctuality was a virtue in those far-off days, and it was said that the neighbours set their clocks and watches by Charles Seabrook's time-keeping. He left for work at precisely the same time every day, and was a familar sight striding past their windows wearing his straw boater in summer and black bowler hat in winter. When gardening and tending his fruit trees he used his old bowler which was kept in the shed behind the house. One day his grandchildren, thinking him safely out of the way, used the hat for target practice in a game of bows and arrows. Charles emerged unexpectedly from the back door and the children froze, but all he said was "I see we have some budding Robin Hoods".

The Seabrook children outside 88 Western Road

No doubt he was proud of his grandchildren, as he was of their parents. But his family life had not been without its sorrows. One of Charles' and Lucy's daughters died in childhood, and their son Billy did not return from World War I. A bright and promising young man, he held the rank of Flight Sergeant in the Royal Flying Corps, but was

tragically killed by a bomb whilst on leave in Boulogne.
Twice during the following years Charles visited the war
cemetery in northern France where Billy lies, and on the
first occasion he returned with a cutting of the Michaelmas
Daisy growing on the grave. He planted this in his garden,
and it flourished so vigorously that he was able to take
further cuttings for many of his relatives. Bet, another
daughter, served during the same war in the Womens
Royal Air Force which had only just been established.

As Charles grew older, less physically demanding work
was found for him in the Tring Park estate offices. As
general factotum he busied himself seeing that the
premises were clean and tidy, and also attended to
'special' tasks. These might involve visiting one of the
estate's tenant farmers who had closed a footpath without
authority, or some similar minor misdeamour where 'a
quiet word' was called for. When Charles finally retired at
the age of 72, he had many memories and tales of the old
Rothschild days. He used to recount that after the family
had returned from the South of France each year, his
Lordship always organised a shooting party in Tring Park.
The keepers were instructed to have sufficient deer
available to provide good sport. The resulting venison
was cut into quarters and distributed to tenants on the
estate, and they could even stipulate which cut they
preferred. Charles always took his share to his daughter
and her family. She then cured the hide in some way, and
cut the skin as a backing for her husband's working
gloves. The same skills were applied to fox hides which
were made into fur stoles. These were given to Charles by
his friend, the Water Bailiff at Tring Reservoirs.

Maybe in old age Charles thought back to when he was a
robust young man of 22, taking part in Tring's 1887
Golden Jubilee Sports held in the Park. Then he was a
fine athlete and won a wall-clock, an inkstand, and a

table, all fitted with a silver plate that commemorated the event. Another later award was a silver medal presented to him for his long service of 20 years with the Second Battalion Bedfordshire Volunteer Regiment.

His fine constitution ensured that he lived into healthy old age, his only real affliction being deafness. He remained keenly interested in current affairs, and his Sunday morning ritual involved a visit to his daughter's house opposite, where he studied the newspaper with the aid of a magnifying glass. (Lucy, a strict Baptist, did not approve of Sunday papers.)

Charles was spared a slow decline into old age, but had a heart attack and died while tending his allotment in Duckmore Lane. No.88 Western Road remained the Seabrook family home until the death of his youngest daughter, Alice, at the age of 96. Over the years, the decorative porch on the house has been replaced, and the ornamental iron railings disappeared in World War II, but the outbuilding at the rear, where Lucy used to launder the Rothschild's clothes, remains intact.

Sources

The Seabrook family
The Bucks Herald archives

Sometimes it is a great advantage to be very small. This was a truth borne out by two toy dogs who sailed with their owners on the maiden voyage of the *Titanic*. Miss Margaret Hayes, aged 24 and travelling alone, was able to carry her Pom into Lifeboat 7, and another lady with a Pom went into Lifeboat 6. Her husband was lost when the ship went down, but we hope that her little dog was some small consolation.

People may have varying opinions on specimens of the Pomeranian breed of dog - either they are seen as a fluffy cuddly bundle, or a bouncy yapping nuisance. The credit or otherwise of their presence in this country can be blamed on Queen Charlotte, the wife of George III. In 1767 she imported two dogs from her native north Germany, and these were seen and admired by one of her neighbours at Kew, the artist Thomas Gainsborough. When the Queen asked him to paint a portrait of her new pets, this brought the breed to the attention of the upper classes.

In late Victorian times, one of Gainsborough's most famous full-length portraits, *The Morning Walk*, appropriately graced the walls of the morning room at Tring Park house. (This picture nows hangs in The National Gallery.) The painting shows a young wealthy couple, dressed in the height of fashion, strolling arm-in-arm round their estate. In the foreground a white Pomeranian devotedly gazes up at them. This dog may not be recognisible to modern eyes, since Poms in the 18th-century weighed up to thirty pounds. Over the years they have been steadily bred down in weight, and the present standard specifies four to five pounds.

'The Morning Walk' in *Tring Park House,* c.1890

The Pomeranian is a member of the hardy Spitz species which originated within the Arctic Circle and was bred to haul sledges, and their original size is understandable. It is not known when the Pom was first brought to Europe, but it found favour in several countries when it was used for herding sheep. Queen Victoria was enchanted with these dogs during a visit to Florence, and returned home with a few examples. She remained deeply attached to the breed, and her dogs were often exhibited in shows. In her later years the Queen's popularity increased, and so did that of her dogs. This started the 'Golden Age' of the Pom and this lasted from 1891, when the Pomeranian Society was founded, until the outbreak of World War I. The cute little dogs provided excellent subject-matter for postcards of the time, and they were depicted in rather sickeningly sentimental, winsome, and 'amusing' poses.

Edwardian postcards

During the Edwardian period, in Tring as everywhere else, Poms were popular pets in many households. One Pom owner in the town who could afford to indulge his hobby was Richardson Carr, Lord Rothschild's formidable Agent at Tring Park estate. This grand gentleman was nicknamed 'The Duke' because of his imperious manner, and also his exalted position that allowed him to influence many facets of Tring life to a quite extraordinary degree.

Until 1908 he lived at the *Home Farm* in Park Road, and then moved to a large new house at No.8 High Street, built for him by his employer. This was no doubt a site chosen as convenient for the Rothschild estate offices that were next door.

Richardson Carr

Richardson's dogs, seldom fewer than ten in number, were kennelled at the *Home Farm*, and tended by Charles Seabrook (the previous Tring Personality). Grooming, feeding, exercising, and whelping activities kept Charles busy, especially when the dogs were exhibited in Paris and other shows on the Continent. (Charles and his wife also owned a Pom known, without too much originality, simply as 'Pom'; this hid under the kitchen range whenever their grandchildren visited.) Richardson Carr's high-standing in the Pom world was demonstrated when he was elected to the Committee of the Pomeranian Society in 1909. By that date, the breed had gained championship status, and Richardson was called upon to act as a judge for the various classes.

Richardson Carr's Pomeranians with Charles Seabrook at the *Home Farm*

Fashion is fickle, and by about 1920 the Pekinese had become more popular than the Pom. Today, Poms are seldom seen outside dog shows; nor for that matter are Pekes. At the time of writing the most popular small dog is the Jack Russell Terrier, probably because, in contrast to the Pom and the Peke, little time needs to be spent in grooming its short coat.

Sources

The Pomeranian Society
The Ultimate Dog Book, David Taylor 1990
A Dog of your own, Joan Palmer 1993

By the age of 43 years George Joseph Smith had married eight times. Seven of these were bigamous unions, and three of his brides had a gruesome, watery end. On Friday 1st July 1915, although defended by the famous Edward Marshall Hall KC, the jury found George Joseph Smith guilty of murder, and he was hanged in Maidstone prison two weeks later. His crimes caused a national sensation, and have always been called the "The Brides in the Bath" case.

Geroge Joseph Smith

What may not be so well known is that the second of his three murder victims was a local girl from Aston Clinton named Alice Flora Burnham. Her parents, Charles and Elizabeth Burnham, were part of a well-established family in that area. One family member owned a grocery and stationery store in the village; another operated as a coal merchant, supplying the L. & N.W. Railway; and a third dealt in hay. At the time of the trial, newspaper editors, never adverse to spicing up a good story, described Charles Burnham as "a wealthy fruit grower". He was in fact not rich, but made a very good living from orchards planted on land in at least six different locations in the Aston Clinton area. He owned some small plots himself, but the main acreage, together with his family house, he rented from the Tring Park estate of Lord Rothschild. Charles also had some income from rents he received for four cottages he had purchased in the village.

Vivacious and buxom Alice trained as a private nurse, and by the age of 25 was living and working in Southsea. For some years she had been nursing an invalid and as her leisure time was limited, she had little opportunity to find herself a boyfriend. Having been reared as a good Methodist, her Sundays were spent attending chapel. If Alice had been less devout she would have been more fortunate, as it was in the Methodist chapel in Southsea that she became aware of an older man in an adjacent pew eyeing her with interest. Alice was flattered and no wonder, for not only was George Smith fashionably dressed and appeared to be well-off, but on acquaintance he proved to be charming and witty.

Born in Bethnal Green in 1872, George used his sharp Cockney wits to make a living from petty crime, and by deceiving unsuspecting women. Prior to marrying his first murder victim, he had already wed once legally and three times bigamously, on each occasion defrauding his brides of their life savings and possessions. His chequered career had included several arrests, followed by spells in gaol. When he then met Beatrice (Bessie) Munday and discovered she lived on income from a capital sum of £2,500 (which would only be released after her death) George lost no time with his wooing. Susceptible Bessie fell for his charms and, despite opposition from her family, married George and settled with him in Herne Bay. Wasting no time, he persuaded her to make a will leaving him everything. George laid his plans carefully - first came the will, then purchase of a bath, followed by a visit with his new wife to the doctor. With a great show of solicitude befitting a newly-married man, George informed the doctor that his wife suffered from fits, although Bessie protested that she did not. It was not long afterwards that the same doctor was summoned urgently to the house in Herne Bay to find Bessie naked in the bath, with her head under water, and dead.

George claimed she must have suffered a fit and drowned, and the jury agreed, for a verdict of death by misadventure was recorded. Naturally all her assets passed to George. The 'grieving' widower may have been surprised by the easy success of his first foray into murder. So much so that, instead of contenting himself with his new fortune, he rapidly determined to select a new victim.

His wedding to Alice Burnham came fifteen months later, but not before he had been taken on a visit to meet her family. The couple journeyed to Tring Station to be greeted by Alice's parents, followed by a drive to their house in the centre of Aston Clinton. The visit could not be described as successful, as Alice's mother and father took an immediate dislike to her new friend. In the following weeks, Charles Burnham became increasingly uneasy and tried hard to persuade her to break off the engagement, declaring to his relatives and others that his future son-in-law appeared "evil looking".

His suspicions were aroused further by George's continual reference to a sum of £104 which was due to Alice. The infatuated girl was adamant that she would marry George and, with reluctance, Charles forwarded the amount, which of course was passed to George, as well as her savings of

£27.9s.5d. The deep unease suffered by her worried parents caused them to contact the police to ask that a check be made on George Joseph Smith. A detective sergeant called to interview him and was not entirely happy; but on his second visit he found the couple away and, fatally for Alice, the matter was not pursued.

In due course George married Alice at Portsmouth Registry Office and, considering it wise to put several miles between them and Buckinghamshire, whisked her off for

Charles Burnham

Alice Burnham

a honeymoon in Blackpool. A comfortable room was found in a lodging house owned by Mr and Mrs Crossley, which George had been at pains to check held the latest modern convenience - an upstairs bathroom. (After all, why change a successful formula?) Like Charles Burnham, the landlords also disliked George, and later when he came to trial Mrs Crossley related her doubts about her lodger.

Apart from the £104, Alice had no appreciable money of her own, and was soon persuaded to insure her life for £500. When she supposedly complained of headaches, the predictable visit to the doctor followed. Just one month after the wedding the newly-weds went for a walk, Alice commenting afterwards that she was tired. George suggested the best remedy for fatigue was a hot bath, and asked Mrs Crossley to run the water. Whilst having tea, the Crossleys noticed water seeping through the ceiling over their heads - obviously the bath was overflowing. At this moment, George appeared in the doorway holding two eggs which he said he had bought for breakfast the next morning. Told about the water, he raced upstairs, wrenched open the bathroom door, and shouted "Fetch the doctor. My wife cannot speak to me!" Dr Billing was soon on the scene, but too late, for Alice was dead and under the water.

Events that followed the tragedy echoed those at Herne Bay. Again an inquest led to a verdict of accidental death from a fit in the bath. Alice Burnham was given the cheapest possible funeral, her body buried in a pauper's grave, and all her possessions were hastily sold.

Very soon George found a second Alice (Reavil) and, before abandoning her, swiftly relieved her of her savings. In less than a year he married again (in Bath!), this time to a wealthy clergyman's daughter, Margaret Lofty, her great attraction for him being her life insurance policy of £700. On this occasion he assumed the name of Lloyd, which was one of several aliases he used for his bigamous unions. Once married, they rented rooms in a house (with a bath of course) in Highgate, London. The following day came the trip to the doctor, who could find nothing wrong with Margaret. Once the couple returned home, George asked the landlady to run a nice hot bath for his wife, and then settled down in the front room to play the harmonium. (The landlady later recalled that the tune had been "Nearer My God to Thee".) A quarter of an hour later a knock on the front door revealed George, who claimed he had "just popped out to get some tomatoes for Mrs Lloyd's supper". He enquired if his wife was out of the bath. Unsurprisingly, she was not, and the pair ascended the stairs to find Margaret drowned. George staged grief-stricken despair, and once again a verdict of death by misadventure was recorded at the inquest.

He must have rubbed his hands at the ease of it all, but had reckoned without one important difference. As the inquest on his third victim was held in London, the incident was reported in national Sunday newspapers, and the story was read by thousands of readers all over the country, including Charles Burnham. He noted at once the similarity of the case to that of the death of Alice, and once more approached the police. Another reader of the story was Mr Crossley, the landlord of the lodging house in Blackpool where Alice had died, and when he also contacted the police, George's fate was sealed. After a lengthy inquiry, his various aliases were discovered, as well as the death of Beatrice Munday. While the murders were being investigated, he was held on a charge of bigamy.

At George's trial the eminent Home Office pathologist, Bernard Spilsbury, took infinite pains to establish that it was impossible to slip under the bath-water accidentally. The jury requested a practical demonstration, and in a side room the police inspector investigating the case acquired a full bath of water and a young lady wearing a bathing costume. He explained Spilsbury's point, and then showed that the victim could be pulled down by lifting the knees with one hand, whilst pushing the head with the other hand. He was carried away by enthusiasm, and pinned his unfortunate volunteer under the water a little too long, and the wretched girl became unconscious and had to be revived. This demonstration convinced the jury, and in only 22 minutes a verdict of guilty was returned.

George Smith was taken to the old prison in Maidstone, the scene of 57 other executions since its beginnings in Georgian times. Here he was despatched by the public hangman who carried out his task with practised efficiency on a Home Office standard-pattern gallows, while George was protesting his innocence to the end. (No doubt his five living 'wives' gave thanks for their amazing good fortune.)

Poor Alice Burnham was the second female from villages near Tring who gained a brief claim to fame by becoming a victim of murder, (see Ruth Osborne, Tring Personality No.15). There the similarity ends, as their stories are in no way alike. It was in old age that Ruth met an humiliating death at the hands of a drunken opportunist; whereas Alice, still young, was murdered by a cynical and ruthless serial killer who preyed on trusting women.

Sources

Buckinghamshire County archives
www.murderuk.com
www.anvil.clara.net
Murder Casebook, Marshall Cavendish Ltd.. 1991
The Brides in the Bath, ITV1, December 2003

HONORABLE SIR HARRY VAISEY 1877 - 1965

Mr Justice Vaisey was the only member of the legal profession born in Tring who rose to become a High Court judge. It is possible that he never wanted to don a black cap over his wig and pronounce the death sentence on a prisoner; nor perhaps did he even wish to send anyone down for a lengthy term. The dramas of the criminal court may not have appealed to him, as his temperament was more suited to the intricacies of the civil courts, and in the Chancery Division of the High Court Harry Vaisey could use his cool analytical brain to its best effect.

His interest in law came from his father, Arthur Vaisey, who as a young solicitor in 1877 set out from Gloucester to find a suitable practice. From three options in different parts of the country, he chose Tring where the town's respected lawyer, John Shugar, had recently died. Arthur borrowed the necessary £700 from his father and joined the existing partner, Shugar junior. Then he moved to Tring with his young wife, and for a short time they accepted the hospitality of the land agent, William Brown, at his house *Beech Grove* in Station Road (see Tring Personality No. 56). When the couple were able to, they transferred to Mr Shugar's old house at No.4 Park Street, and there Harry, the first of their nine children, was born.

Holly Field, c.1900

Then a long love affair began between the Vaisey family and Tring. Arthur eventually practised under his sole name, and was still doing so many years later when he died at the age of 88. He had no resources except what he earned, but as both his business and his family grew, and his finances improved, he decided to have a house built for him on the outskirts of Tring. He was well pleased with the comfortable residence in the currently fashionable Arts & Crafts style, embellished with tile-hanging, gables, and ornate chimneys, which William Huckvale, the local architect, designed. Finished in 1882 and named *Holly Field*, this became the family's much-loved home, and a notable centre of affection, hospitality, and friendship. *Holly Field* has since been demolished, but its name lives on at the original site.

Always proud of his adopted town, and also of Hertfordshire, Arthur once received an envelope addressed to him at "Tring, Bucks", which he returned promptly to the sender and marked it "Not known". He became very skilled in the knowledge of Tring's history and traditions, and for 50 years he served the town as Clerk to the Council.

The achievements of his eldest son, Harry, also gave Arthur reason for parental pride for he had proved a brillant scholar at Shrewsbury School, and in 1885 he won a Brasenose Scholarship, worth £100 a year for five years at Hertford College, Oxford. There he obtained his First in moderations, and two years later his name appeared in the first-class honours of the Oxford Classical 'Greats' list.

Harry's success continued, and in 1901 he was called to the Bar at Lincoln's Inn. Two years later he married Eleonora, the daughter of Reverend Quennell, vicar of Tring. As a barrister, Harry was qualified to act as advocate in all courts of law, and from then onwards he steadily progressed up the judicial ladder, a major step coming in 1925 when he was appointed King's Counsel. In court he then wore robes of silk and sat within the bar of the law courts. Harry's style of advocacy was described as thorough and persuasive, and his pleasant courteous manner and dry humour made him a popular figure with his colleagues at the Bar, and even with the judges.

Mr Justice Vaisey

Progress in the legal profession does not always come easily, and Harry had to wait until 1944 for appointment as judge in the Chancery Division of the High Court of Justice. When the announcement came it was somewhat unexpected as, at the age of 66, he had been passed over several times in favour of younger men, although he was always recognised as a learned authority on ecclesiastical law. When it came, his promotion was regarded as a well-deserved reward to a sound and capable lawyer of high character, and could be relied upon to maintain the highest traditions of the Bench. His knighthood followed almost at once after his promotion.

Tring lost no time in calling upon its distinguished townsman. During World War II, strenuous efforts were made to increase National Savings and most towns staged a 'Salute the Soldier' week. Harry was invited to share the platform on Church Square with the actress, Peggy Ashcroft (Tring Personality No.34), and he made a stirring speech, very much in the Churchillian tradition.

Harry's sister, Margaret, who was Chairman of Tring Council presided at the event. It is an interesting point that she was unmarried, as were three of her sisters, for their father, a true product of the Victorian age, had forbidden them to wed the men of their choice, as he considered that none of them were worthy of his daughters.   Three other daughters did however 'escape' to marry. Harry had only one brother, Roland, also a solicitor, and he was killed in the Great War.

When peace came after World War II, Judge Vaisey continued on his distinguished way, his progress being marked by many responsible appointments in fields other than the law. Two of these especially must have given him great satisfaction when he became an honorary fellow of Hertford College, and was also appointed as treasurer of Lincoln's Inn. In 1966 he and his wife, Eleonora, celebrated their Diamond Wedding, an event tinged with sadness, as one of their two children had already died.

Harry Vaisey lived until the great age of 92, and was buried in Tring Cemetery: later a thanksgiving service for his life was held in the Chapel of Lincoln's Inn. His wife lived on to be 100 and, surrounded by the Vaisey family, she enjoyed a celebratory luncheon party.

Sources

Hertfordshire Countryside, Summer 1960
The Times, November 1965
The Bucks Herald archives
Encyclopædia Britannica
Who was Who, 1961-1981

In November 1962 Tring's Building and Town Planning Committee agreed that *Beech Grove*, a large empty house in Station Road, could be used as offices by the British Trust for Ornithology, where some 12 people were to be employed. This early-Victorian white stucco house, the first property to be built in the road, was erected for his family by William Brown, Tring's land agent and brother of brewer John Brown (Tring Personality No.1). William took advantage of a scheme by the newly-founded London to Birmingham Railway Company to encourage building near their stations. In return he received a novel gift - a free first-class rail pass for 21 years between Tring and Euston.

Beech Grove, c.1997

As early as 1927, a group of ornithologists had proposed that a national Bird Census be undertaken, similar to such projects in other countries. The Oxford Bird Census was set up, and from these small beginnings the British Trust for Ornithology developed. This was an independent, scientific research trust, investigating the population, movements, and ecology of wild birds in the British Isles.

One of the main aims was to encourage volunteers of all ages, and from all walks of life, to improve their bird-watching skills and to contribute to surveys undertaken by the Trust.

In 1962 as the BTO's activities were consolidated, the main office at Oxford and the Ringing Unit at the British Museum were moved to *Beech Grove*. Tring was the natural choice of location, as at that time the ringing tags used by the BTO carried the address of the Natural History Museum, a branch of which was the Zoological Museum in Akeman Street. The task of seeking suitable premises was given to Chris Mead, who had joined the BTO staff a year previously. It so happened that Chris had deep roots in Tring, and could trace his Mead family tree as far back as the 1560s. In the late-Victorian period one of his forebears had moved away to Brighton to establish a successful grocery and provision shop. Chris's own father became a master grocer, but neither of his sons was interested in following the family business: in any case, Chris's brilliance at mathematics ensured him a university place.

After education at Aldenham School, he studied at Peterhouse, Cambridge, but never finished his degree. His interest in the natural world led him to seek a job where his skills and tremendous enthusiasm could be put to good use. Throughout his adult life the adjective always applied to Chris was 'big', which fully described both his stature and personality. Never half-hearted about his interests, he brought the same energy to his various hobbies as he did to his work. His pastimes included listening to jazz, watching rugby, motor racing, local history, and archæology.

Chris and his wife, Verity, met whilst both working at the BTO in Tring, and in due course they moved to a house with a large garden in Beaconsfield Road. In 1964 this property had been bequeathed by its owner, Herbert Stevens, to the British Ornithologists' Club, with the proviso that the Club had to use it for its own purposes or let it to a Member as a furnished house. This generous benefactor, a tea planter in India, had indulged his hobby of natural history by undertaking several intrepid collecting expeditions to the Himalayas and New Guinea. He wrote a book about his longest journey called "Through Deep Defiles to the Tibetan Uplands", a title evoking columns of loaded yaks, and visits to remote Buddist monasteries, and even the possible thrilling discovery of Yeti footprints in the snow. After these adventures, when Herbert Stevens and his wife retired to their house in Tring, they brought with them many souvenirs of their travels which were 'inherited' by the Mead family. These included seven cases of stuffed birds in the front room, and a buffalo's head in the loft.

With a firm base in Tring of both home and job, Chris was able to concentrate fully on his passion for birds, and he worked for more than 40 years at the BTO, of which 33 were spent in the Ringing Unit. It is estimated that he caught and ringed over 400,000 birds of 350 species, and in the process travelled to 18 countries. He acquired an encyclopædic knowledge of bird migration and habits, and employed his mathematical mind to the compilation of the necessary statistical surveys. Keen to pass on his findings, and to encourage other ornithologists, Chris developed outstanding communicating skills, and that led him to become the Trust's most popular ambassador.

He regularly contributed to many BBC natural history programmes, including "The Living World" on Radio 4, and several times appeared on national television. On one occasion a television crew visited the Mead family's back garden to film an item for the children's programme "Blue Peter". Other initiatives included boosting the Trust's funds by devising a CD of nightingale song to support an appeal on behalf of the species. He also found time to contribute to and to write many books on birds and their migration and was particularly proud of one of his volumes - "The State of the Nation's Birds", published in the millennium year 2000. His services to the world of birds did not go unrecognised, and he was one of the very few people to be honoured by all three main bird organisations of the UK. In the three years between 1996 and 1999 he was presented with the medal of the British Ornithologist's Union; the Bernard Tucker medal for services to the BTO; and the RSPB medal for his achievements in the causes of wild bird protection and countryside conservation.

Tring people enjoyed spotting this local celebrity. Hard to ignore, by virtue of his stature and imposing beard, Chris was a familar sight driving round the town in his Land Rover. He was prevailed upon to serve a term on the Town Council from 1987 to 1991, but how this task was added to his multitude of other activities is a mystery. In 1991 everything changed as, due to pressure of space and after 30 years at *Beech Grove*, the BTO announced relocation plans and removal to Norfolk. The premises chosen are known as *The Nunnery*, a large house once occupied by Lord Nelson's grandmother. It was necessary for many of the staff, including the Mead family, to leave Tring and start a new life in Thetford.

Chris Mead

Beech Grove was acquired by a developer who planned to demolish the house and erect six detached homes on the site. This suggestion drew protests from residents living nearby, and an attempt was made to block the proposal by setting up the *Beech Grove* Action Group, which sent a 100-signature petition to Dacorum Borough Council. The Council fully supported the residents throughout their campaign and, in an attempt to pre-empt demolition of the house, requested that the property should be given recognised Grade II listing. This application was rejected by the Secretary of State for National Heritage, who stated "this building is not original enough or sufficiently well preserved to warrant listing". Accordingly, six years after the departure of the BTO, stately and shabby old *Beech Grove* was pulled down and only the gate-pillars were spared.

By this time, Chris Mead's ill health had brought about his early, and supposed, 'retirement', after which he became the Trust's press consultant, regularly interviewed on the radio and by newspapers and journals. He died suddenly and peacefully in his sleep, causing great sorrow not only to his wife, Verity, and their three daughters, but to the legion of his fans in the bird world. A celebration of his life was held at the Trust's Thetford headquarters when over 250 friends and former colleagues gathered to share their memories of a unique man. Shortly afterwards, the BBC's "Nature" series paid its own tribute, and in a programme about nightingales Chris was fondly recalled when the presenter talked of his pioneering work. The programme included a dusk chorus of nightingales, as well as extracts from the CD that Chris had compiled.

Amazed by the spontaneous out-pouring of sympathy following his death, his family and the Trust decided to commemorate Chris in a special way. It was decided that a fund should be launched to develop the Chris Mead

Library at the headquarters of the British Trust for
Ornithology in Thetford. Donations flowed in from all
over the country, and the fund-raising manager was
quoted as saying "people really appreciated how Chris
could explain bird behaviour and migration in a way
which was both understandable and awe-inspiring". There
is a plaque in the library which reads

This library is dedicated to the memory of Chris Mead (1940-2003)
who inspired BTO birdwatchers and ringers for more than 40 years.
A man of ideas, enthusiasm, and exceptional knowledge."

Sources

www.bto.org
www.fact-index.com
The Bucks Herald archives
The Gazette, January 1997
Bulletin of the British Ornithologists' Club, December 1991
That Tring Air, Arthur Macdonald 1940
The Walter Rothschild Zoological Museum

There are many ways to become well known. Robert Stephenson (Tring Personality No.43) spent his life making travel easier. His determination to succeed finally overcame all the fierce opposition, and without his resolve modern trains would not have appeared until decades later. Merely by their own outrageously evil acts, some can even make others noteworthy. A classic example was Alice Burnham (Tring Personality No.54), when George Smith drowned her in a domestic bath. Some achieve local fame because of outstanding valour. James Osborne (Tring Personality No.4) won a Victoria Cross by saving a comrade under intense enemy fire.

There are other ways to become well known and even a Personality. Consider the case of Edward Cockayne. Imagine the picture brought to mind if one thinks of an elderly bachelor living alone in an over-large house, whose companions are hundreds of caterpillars in jars. The average person may find this scenario bizarre, and perhaps a little pathetic. But there is still more to tell; much more.

Edward Alfred Cockayne came from a comfortable family background in Sheffield, educated at Charterhouse, then at Balliol College, Oxford, earning a first-class degree in Natural Sciences. His medical education continued at St.Bartholomew's, where he won a Brackenbury Scholarship for Medicine, and in 1909 he passed the examination to become a member of the Royal College of Physicians. He has been described as a bird-like, slightly-built man, but with an unpredictable temper.

Graduating as Doctor of Medicine in 1912, Edward was appointed medical registrar and, later, physician to out-patients at the Middlesex Hospital. He then joined the staff of the Victoria Hospital for Children, an early experience that set the scene for what was to be his life-long interest in paediatrics.

Dr Edward Cockayne

After a short period as house physician at Bart's, he moved to the Hospital for Sick Children, Great Ormond Street, and this appointment set the pattern for Edward's path in life. His career was interrupted from 1915 to 1919, during which time he served in the Royal Navy, and was based in Archangel at the time of the Russian Revolution. When he returned to London he started to progress in his chosen career, and in 1928 was elected vice-president in the section dealing with diseases of children. Four years later he was appointed full physician at Great Ormond Street.

Earlier at this hospital, Edward had served as a junior to

the geneticist Sir Archibald Garrod, an eminent physician who had studied every unusual genetic aberration found in the young, especially the disorders of the ductless glands. He encouraged Edward to share in and explore this field of medicine. Edward's results led him to his life's other great passion - entomology. He began to specialise in the genetic variations of British butterflies and moths, and he compared the unusual manifestions in this field with many of the genetic abnormalities that he investigated as a paediatrician. This complex work made it almost inevitable that he found his way to the Zoological Museum at Tring. Working closely with Doctor Karl Jordan (Tring Personality No.16) his contribution to entomology was quickly recognised, and he was elected President of the Royal Entomological Society in 1943. Two years later Edward took the decision to make Tring his permanent home. He may have been helped in this by the offer of *The Oasis*, No. 8 High Street - an imposing house originally built for Lord Rothschild's agent, and on the face of it, much too large for one quiet middle-aged bachelor.

Although he now spent more time on his hobby, his professional work-load did not diminish. In the year that he came to Tring he undertook the task of consultant physician at the Middlesex Hospital, and also a similar job at Great Ormond Street. He was in fact one of the last physicians to combine this work with paediatric practice. Edward also published over 200 papers and books on his specialist subjects, the most important being "Inherited Abnormalities of the Skin and its Appendages" which The Lancet described as "an immense amount of labour spread over many years".

Two years after Edward's arrival in Tring he offered his entomological collection to the Natural History Museum. He was invited to combine this with the existing British collections, which included those of the late Walter Rothschild. At the same time he became assistant curator at the Tring Museum, and amalgamated both sources. The combined collection was then the complete range of variation known within each species, and everything about their genetics. Edward constantly supplemented this revision with rare and beautiful specimens at his own expense, and he encouraged valuable donations from others, until the collection then numbered 50,000 examples. In 1954 Edward may have welcomed his retirement from medicine, for he was then able to devote his whole attention to entomology.

Perhaps his dedication to science had not allowed Edward time for interest in the opposite sex, for he never married. Descriptions of his personality seem to imply that his academic work held greater attraction for him than human relationships. This is strange in a man who must surely have needed to establish rapport with his child patients in order to get the best results. His colleagues agreed that Edward was a superb diagnostician, but with little interest in undergraduate teaching, and this further suggests that he was emotionally self-sufficient, or perhaps simply shy. This seems to be proven by the fact that he had many acquaintances and admirers, but no close friends. Even so, he may have inspired affection amongst his colleagues at the Museum, for there he was known by the nickname 'Cocky'. In his later years the one person upon whom he most depended was his housekeeper at *The Oasis*, May Paisley (née Digweed), whose family lived at No. 27 Henry Street in Tring.

Seeing beautiful butterflies and moths impaled on pins in a glass case is not to everyone's taste, but the work carried out by Edward Cockayne is now known to have contributed greatly to the interpretation of genetic abnormalities. This was recognised in 1954 when he was awarded the OBE in the Queen's Birthday Honours, for services to entomology. Edward's ill-health prevented him attending this investiture and the decoration had to be sent on, together with a letter from the Queen that she was sorry not to have been able to present it in person.

The Oasis, No. 8 High Street, Tring

His housekeeper, May, had nursed her husband at *The Oasis* during his final illness, and three years later she faced a similar hard time as Edward's death approached. (When he became too ill to look after his huge collection of caterpillars, she also tended the jars for him.) He was a heavy smoker, even taking his pipe into the bath, and this no doubt intensified the emphysema that had incapacitated him towards the end of his life. Five years before his death Edward had set up the Cockayne Trust with the object of encouraging the study of the science of entomology, and at the same time endowed £1,000 a year to fund the Cockayne Research Fellowship which promoted new work on lepidoptera. In his will he left a considerable amount of money to the British Museum, together with his watercolours. Other amounts and his books were bequeathed to various entomological societies. Further sums were left to the Royal College of Physicians and the Royal Society of Medicine, which honoured him by opening the Cockayne Suite in 1963. His name also lives on in the field of his specialist subject of paediatrics. The Cockayne Syndrome is a rare inherited disorder, that is due to a defect in the cells that normally repair DNA. Sufferers are sensitive to sunlight, usually of short stature, and often age prematurely.

The story of this unusual man, Edward Cockayne, cannot be concluded without mentioning that he did not forget May Paisley, his devoted housekeeper. From his will she received a generous inheritance - sufficient to purchase a small house in Beaconsfield Road for her retirement.

Sources

The Cockayne Trust
The Bucks Herald archives
www.whonamedit.com

All who have ever been to sea know that every ship has its own distinct character, but it seems strange that a small town, almost in the middle of the country, should have any vessel among its Personalities. In fact during the two major conflicts of the 20th century three different ships linked Tring to the navy. HMS *Tring* has in fact little connection with the town other than its name, but it is thought that this mine sweeper was called *Tring* when the Navy ran out of suitable names of towns which could be understood readily when calling over the radio. It might be that a member of the crew came from the area, and suggested it as a short easily-transmitted word.

Although it was known that a ship named *Tring* had been part of the fleet during World War I, nothing further could be discovered until recently. An appeal for information in the Parish Magazine, as long ago as the 1930s, brought no response. But a chance find by Michelle Warden of a sailor's hat ribbon in an antiques shop in London in 2001, led her to try and determine the origin of her purchase by asking her father to carry out some research. The results revealed the facts about HMS *Tring*, and later Michelle gave the hat ribbon to the town and it is now in the ownership of the Local History Society. When the local paper reported this find, the article caught the attention of Phyllis Proctor of Long Marston, whose father had served in the Navy during World War I. Although not on the *Tring*, he had sent home two photographs of the ship and her crew, and Phyllis had kept them in an album.

One of the postcards shows the entire crew mustered in front of the ship's funnel, Fresh-faced youngsters smile confidently at the camera, while older bearded crew members appear more solemn.

The crew of HMS *Tring*

Tring was built on the Clyde by Simmons of Renfrew, and commissioned on 23rd August 1918. Designed as Role 1 Mine Sweeper, and Role 2 Hunt Class ship, with a crew of more than 60, her first purpose was to search, find, and blow up mines laid in the English Channel by the enemy. She was part of the 6th Flotilla Fleet and under the charge of Commander Jack Dalrymple Walters (1897-1981). At that time, mine sweeping involved two slow-moving vessels steaming abreast, towing a sweeping wire which was kept at the required depth by a wooden 'kite' or 'otter'. The design of these devices ensured a downward pull on the wire, and as the mines were swept to the surface they were destroyed. Often this operation had to be carried out under enemy fire.

Before World War I all maritime powers made public announcements where they had laid minefields so that neutral shipping could avoid them. But when the Germans broke maritime custom, flew neutral flags, and laid mines from ships off the Suffolk coast, in the Humber,

Tyne, and other areas, the British government also abandoned strict observance of international law. Within a month of the outbreak of war, 250 trawlers, drifters and patrol vessels were countering the German mine offensive. Clearing minefields imposes a great strain on the resources of any country whose waters are mined, since this operation needs many special vessels and a highly trained personnel.

HMS *Tring*

Naturally it was a hazardous and nerve-racking operation, and many such ships did not survive. Mine-clearing activities in European waters were necessary for a further two years after the war ended, and *Tring* safely weathered her tour of duty. In 1920 she was ready for other work, and that year saw her in Queens Town (now called Cork) in Ireland on patrol duties. This entailed work for the

Patrol and Fishery Protection Flotilla, often bringing supplies to coastguard stations. The following year saw a special mission, transporting convicts from Dun Laoghaire to Plymouth.

Later that same year *Tring* was commissioned as a sea-going tender to the shore establishment HMS *Ganges* in Slotley Point, near Ipswich, a Royal Naval Training Centre for Boys. For the next four years she was commanded by three different officers, all holding the rank of Lieutenant Commander. It is estimated that about 7,000 boys had their first experience of man-o-war routine on the *Tring*. A less enviable distinction for her and her crew was that most of these 7,000 experienced that distressing motion malady peculiar to the sea.

Owing to the need for economy, in August 1925 she was put into reserve to HMS *Blenheim*, a depot ship at Sheerness in the Isle of Sheppey. The gallant and useful little ship HMS *Tring* ended her life where she was born - on the Clyde. On 7th October 1927 she was sold for scrap to the Alloa Ship-Breaking Company in Glasgow.

Sources

Liddell Hart Centre for Military Archives
www.hmsganges.asoc.org
www.aim.25.ac.uk
The Berkhamsted Gazette, April and May 2001
Chamber's Encyclopædia

In World War II HMS *Aeolus* never floated on water (not even on the canal or the River Bulbourne!) for *Aeolus* was a land ship based in Tring at Nos. 51 and 52 High Street.

These days the premises are Metcalfe's hardware shop; here we can browse and buy anything from a paintbrush to a designer teapot. The buildings are a great deal older than they appear from the frontage, and in Victorian times were occupied firstly by Tompkins, then Dawes, both ironmongers. From the 1920s until just before the war, this pattern was broken when they became Robins & Marriott garage, with a showroom for Wolseley cars. Around 1937 the business was bought by Flying Officer Buxton, a retired flying instructor at deHavilland's aircraft factory; and he added a restaurant on the first floor. When the war began, Buxton was recalled for duty, and the premises requisitioned by the Admiralty for war work. Shortly afterwards *Aeolus* was established in Tring, run by a RNR Commander with a crew of nearly 50.

AUTOMOBILE ENGINEERS

Skilled Repairs
Coach Painting
Contract Hire

HOUSE LIGHTING PLANTS

Petter Agents
OIL ENGINES
Power Mowers
WIRELESS SETS
and Accessories of all kinds.

Modern Automobile Service.   *Transport.*

ROBINS & MARRIOTT
Telephone 67   **TRING**   *Telegrams " Motors "*

The premises requisitioned by HMS *Aeolus*

The Admiralty's fanciful choice of name for Tring's land ship was logical, as wind power supplied the vital element for the products made. In Roman mythology Aeolus was the keeper of the winds, and lived on the floating rocky island of Liprara, close to Sicily. Ancient peoples believed that Zeus, the king of the gods, gave the winds to Aeolus, and he kept them confined in a cave on a mountain to release whenever he wished. (Aeolus plays an important part in Homer's two great epic poems. In "The Odyssey", he gives the hero a leather bag containing all the winds that could prevent him from sailing home, but when his sailors open the bag which they hope contains treasure, the winds escape and blow the ship off course. In "The Aeneid" the goddess Juno tells Aeolus to cause gales to wreck the fleet of the Trojan king.) Tring folk seemed to care little for the classical connection, and the premises soon became known simply as 'the depot'.

In the early stages of the war large box-kites of bamboo struts were constructed here, packed in canvas bags, delivered to various naval dockyards, and fitted to merchant ships as protection against low-flying attacking aircraft. The taut steel cables attaching the kites to the ships swayed with every breeze, and it was known that enemy pilots feared these greatly. This defensive device was also unpopular with our our own airmen, as a steep descent through low cloud could mean an unexpected encounter needing prompt evasive action.

The kites were later replaced by canvas barrage balloons sent to vulnerable sites in the UK and abroad. As the war progressed, balloon units came into being all over England, some staffed by women trained at the old airship centre at Cardington in Bedfordshire.

Balloon girls in training

Balloons at heights of three- to four-thousand feet formed a barrier to enemy bomber planes, and in the lead-up to D-Day the Americans said "with all the men, tanks, trucks, airplanes, and the tons of supplies being gathered for the invasion, if it hadn't been for the barrage balloons, Britain would have sunk". Later in the war, an even larger barrage was created in the south and east of England when Hitler launched his V1 flying-bomb offensive.

Tring's wartime production increased rapidly and more space was needed. Some balloons were kept in the old stables at Tring Park mansion, with naval ratings billeted above the store. Balloons designated for RAF use were housed in an old storeroom owned by the Zoological Museum on the corner of Akeman and Albert Streets, and a repair centre was set up in a Nissen hut behind the present-day Market Garage in Brook Street. Here damaged balloons were inflated, allowing staff to walk inside and make good with special glue any tears and punctures. Some interiors were fitted with circular wire-mesh screens to confuse enemy Radar; these balloons were attached to barges and towed back and forth along the English Channel. Balloons for use on ships had a small bomb fixed on the cable. When an aircraft collided with a balloon, the bomb slid down and the resulting explosion, hopefully, blew the wings off the plane. These bombs were stored both in the outbuildings at the depot, and at the Stud Farm in Duckmore Lane.

The hand-winches which hoisted balloons into place were packed into wooden crates which were manufactured in a disused building at the *Home Farm*. The assembled bulky items were transported to Tring Station and stored in the sidings. Despatch could either be direct by rail or on one of the five vehicles kept at the depot.

The *Aeolus* crew found time for play as well as work, and entered enthusiastically into the social life of the town. A report of the time tells of a dance at the Victoria Hall, decorated in jaunty nautical style, with Commander Boorman acting as Master of Ceremonies and Lieutenant Kenshaw as auctioneer; he managed to coax the sum of £1.11s.6d. for a cake. The throng of dancers enjoyed the rhythm set by a RAF band, and a refreshment buffet provided by a team of ladies (although quite what tasty delicacies could be provided during this period of strict food rationing is not specified). A satisfactory wartime sum of £25 was raised in aid of the King George Fund for Merchant Sailors, a charity much in the news at a time when the desperate Battle of the Atlantic was at its height. The young people of Tring were not forgotten either, as the crew hosted Christmas parties for children in the upstairs room of the depot.

Some of the crew of HMS *Aeolus*, Commander Boorman R.N.R. in centre

It was not until 4th March 1946 that *Aeolus* was 'paid off' and said goodbye to the town. At a ceremony at the *Rose & Crown* the officers, ratings, and wrens received Tring's official expression of farewell and appreciation. As a token of her wartime presence in the town, two white ensigns were presented by Commander Boorman to the Council and to the Parish Church. He commented that balloons made in Tring had helped to protect over 500 merchant ships, and to bring down 200 doodle-bugs and rockets during the later stages of the war. He further explained that the work of the establishment would be transferred to Southampton, but he and his wife had grown so fond of Tring that they were planning to make it their home. (It is hoped that a good home was found for the *Aeolus* mascot, a talking jackdaw.)

The mascot of *Aeolus* and his minder

After the war the building at Nos. 51 and 52 High Street again became a garage and taxi service business until purchased in 1948 by Metcalfes. For a while reminders of *Aeolus* lingered, including signs on doors which read 'Quartermaster' and 'Petty Officer', but soon everything was gone except the memories of the Tring people who served there, and of the children invited to 'the depot' at Christmas.

Sources

The Bucks Herald archives
Chamber's Encyclopædia
Brewer's Phrase & Fable, 1993

During World War II, Warship Weeks were organised by the National War Savings Committee. It was hoped that villages might each contribute £25,000 to sponsor a motor torpedo-boat, and a city £2m. for a battleship. A realistic figure for a small town was estimated at £62,000, and in March 1942 Tring's Warship Week was opened officially on Church Square by Air Vice Marshall MacEwen, air officer in command at Halton. He was supported in his appeal by Lady Davidson MP, and the actress Peggy Ashcroft (Tring Personality No.34), at that time living in Tring with her baby whilst her husband was serving in the Royal Navy.

The objective encouraged people to invest in National Savings, and also fund-raising by organising social events in Tring and the surrounding villages. Dances, parades, whist drives, and sales-of-work all helped towards the goal, with the added bonus of giving pleasure and boosting morale. The campaign took off, and in the short space of one week the required total was easily exceeded, a sum of £77,113 having been raised.

HMS *Arctic Hunter*

This was more than sufficient for the sponsorship, and *Capel*, the vessel chosen, was a trawler of 365 tons, with a working speed of 10.9 knots. She had been built in 1929 by Cook, Welton & Gemmell of Beverley in Yorkshire for F & T Ross of Hull, using her for fishing work until she was requisitioned by the Admiralty in August 1939. The ship was renamed *Arctic Hunter* and given the pennant number FY 1614, and the suitable emblem of a polar bear. Adapted for mine-sweeping, she carried one 12-lb. gun and two 0.5 calibre Vickers machine guns. Whether or not the endemic fishy smell was eradicated from the ship is not known, but doubtless it was a very unimportant consideration compared to other factors of life on a small vessel in the freezing and hazardous waters of the North Sea and the English Channel.

The vessel was principally involved in the clearance of magnetic mines, which were designed to be actuated by the magnetism of the target cutting the lines of force of a permanent magnet in the mine. The ship *Arctic Hunter* would have been demagnetised by having electrically charged wires wound round the hull, and the sweep involved towing astern an electrically-charged sweep wire which fired at the mines as it passed over them. Mines which came to the surface were destroyed by *Arctic Hunter's* gun, and by the end of the war she was credited with the destruction of 110 mines and a Dornier 217 bomber of the German Luftwaffe. *Arctic Hunter* was also involved in mine clearance operations prior to and during the Allied invasion of Europe on D-Day.

Mine-sweeping was a dangerous and unpleasant task at all times, but especially in winter months. Accordingly, once the money was raised it was announced that Tring would officially adopt the ship, and the local branch of the British Legion was approached to see if a committee could be formed to supply the crewmen with 'woollen comforts'.

They were grateful for the town's efforts, and also for the gifts and books which were sent at Christmas. Commemorative plaques were exchanged between *Arctic Hunter* and the Council chamber in Tring.

In 1944 Mrs Harding of Frogmore Street told the local paper that she had received a letter from her husband, Leading Seaman Norman Harding, in which he said that quite by chance his ship drew alongside *Arctic Hunter* at a port but which he could not name for reasons of security. When the twenty crew members found that he came from Tring they gave him a hearty welcome and invited him aboard, where he was introduced to the Commanding Officer, and shown over the ship. One crew member at the time was Seaman Gunner Alfred Emery, who saw continuous service on *Arctic Hunter* until January 1945, when he was Mentioned in Despatches for distinguished service, having already been awarded the Silver Minesweeper Badge.

'Warship Week' was not the only fund-raising event that was Government-sponsored during the war. As early as May 1941 Tring held a 'War Weapons Week' to raise money for Spitfires. Organised by the National Savings movement, it accompanied a salvage drive where aluminium pots and pans, as well as rags and bones, were collected from the town's households. At the same time, many private properties lost their iron railings, and even the ornate gates which graced the three entrance drives to Tring Park mansion had to be sacrificed. Few people objected, for this seemed of little account compared with the life-and-death struggle being waged overhead in the Battle of Britain. In 1945 when it was all over, post-war austerity replaced wartime shortages, so there was no question that the fancy gates should be refitted at the mansion entrances.

However, certain things did return to normal pre-war use, and *Arctic Hunter* was one of them. Her guns were abandoned and she regained her trawling nets when decommissioned in May 1945. Yet again she acquired a new name - *Lord Foyle* - and continued to operate until 1952, when she was sold for scrap to the British Iron and Steel Corporation. Later that year she was moved to Sunderland to be broken up.

The memento of the wartime service of *Arctic Hunter* still hangs in Tring's Council Offices. A shield-shaped plaque carries the insignia of the mine-sweeping service, and the inscription reads:

"Presented by
The Lords of the Admiralty
to Tring
Urban District Council
to commemorate the adoption of
H.M.S. *Arctic Hunter*
during Warship Week March 1942"

Sources

The Bucks Herald archives
Chambers Encyclopædia

Crew members on the wheelhouse of *Arctic Hunter*

The great George Washington does not appear to have attached very much importance to his roots in England - no doubt he had more pressing matters to occupy his mind. He is on record as saying that genealogy "is of little moment". In reply to an enquiry about his ancestors he stated "in the year 1657, or thereabouts, and during the usurpation of Oliver Cromwell, two brothers John and Lawrence Washington emigrated from the north of England, and settled at Brides Creek on Potomac River .... from whom they were descended, I am possessed of no document to ascertain". However George had his facts rather muddled, for it is true that his family originated in the north of England, but then settled in Sulgrave in Northamptonshire, and later still in Tring. Research carried out long after his death proved that in fact the two brothers mentioned did come from Tring. Even if this information had been available to him, it is unlikely that George would have bothered to find the town on a map. Some modern Americans think differently, and it is not unusual to see them perusing the Washington family tree on the north wall of Tring Church.

George Washington
(1732-1790)

In 1619 Lawrence Washington of Sulgrave, after teaching at Oxford University, left the city and made his way to London. About this time it is thought he met his future bride, Amphyllis Twigden, step-daughter of Andrew Knowling of Tring. Andrew originated from Devon and had made a modest fortune in London as a maker of beaver-fur hats. After accumulating sufficient money, he decided to move to the healthy air of Hertfordshire, and to pursue the life of a country gentleman. His wealth ensured him a reasonable social status, and he was soon fully accepted into Tring life and served as a church warden, donating a parchment-bound volume for use as the parish register. He also willingly undertook his responsibilities as step-father to his wife's children, and later to his Washington grandchildren.

It is possible that Lawrence Washington and Amphyllis Twigden first met at Pendley, owned by a kinsman of Lawrence whom he is known to have visited from time to time. Once married, Lawrence did not turn out to be an entirely satisfactory husband, or a good provider for his three sons and three daughters. In 1633 he was installed as rector of Purleigh in Essex, but Laudian traits and possibly a fondness for the bottle resulted in his ejection from this comfortable living. He spent his last ten years in poverty as vicar of the small parish of Little Braxted. It is thought likely that Amphyllis and the children did not accompany him, for it is recorded that she returned to Tring to care for her widowed step-father after the death of her mother, buried in Tring in 1637. The baptisms of three of Amphyllis's children, Lawrence, Elizabeth, and William, are listed in the registers of Tring Parish, and it is likely that the other three, John, Margaret, and Martha, were baptised in Purleigh, but no records survive. John was the great-grandfather of George Washington, and his exact date of birth is not known.

Possessed of a strong personality, Amphyllis shouldered responsibilty for the upbringing of her family. She also fought for her husband's rights, on behalf of the children, and pursued a claim for some compensation when he was ejected from his living at Purleigh. Her tenacity eventually reaped rewards as, after an appearance before the Cromwellian Standing Committee at Essex, she succeeded in obtaining one-fifth of the value of the tithes and other profits from the benefice of the parish.

Eight years later Amphyllis's step-father, the kindly Andrew Knowling, died and was buried in Tring. His estate was valued at £534.11s.8d., and after legacies of £1 each to the poor of Tring and Wilstone, and 10s. to the poor of Wigginton (who for some reason he felt were less deserving), he left £60 to Amphyllis and various sums to other relatives. His freehold lands and the residue of his estate were inherited by the younger Lawrence, his godson, and obvious favourite.

Although the site of Andrew Knowling's house in Tring is not known for certain, it was probably in the Frogmore or Dundale area. The inventory of his estate and his worldly goods paint a picture of how Amphyllis and the children lived. They resided not in luxury, but in a comfortable fashion far removed from the lot of most folk in the parish. The house boasted such amenities as a cellar for brewing the domestic beer, an outside dairy house with cows and heifers, and a disused mill which was used for storing lumber and wood. The kitchen was well stocked with a dripping pan, a chaffing dish, meat roasters, platters, plates, six old kittles (*sic*), trenchers and even 12 silver spoons, as well as other items. Also listed are "one great wicker chayre, three old litle wicker chayres"; 18 pairs of sheets; nine pillows; nine tableclothes; seven towels; and six dozen napkins. Andrew may have been something of a sportsman, as "a birdinge piece and dagger" are included in the inventory among the sundry items.

A secure home ensured that Amphyllis and her children remained in Tring, and the boys were educated locally, but life was sometimes a struggle and her ambitions for her children had to be pitched at a modest level. William, her youngest son, was apprenticed to a weaver in London for a term of seven years, and Amphyllis endeavoured to find a place for Margaret as a servant, whilst Elizabeth married a blacksmith. When she died intestate, Amphyllis had little or no property of her own. She was buried at Tring on 19th January 1654.

After the death of their mother the family began to break up. In 1657 John Washington, after settling his mother's affairs, gained proficiency as a seaman and worked his way to America on the vessel *Sea Horse of London*. From then on John's story becomes part of the history of the state of Virginia, as he acquired a public position in the colony, and his varied interests included a tobacco plantation, a sawmill, and a gristmill. He married the daughter of a well-to-do Marylander and fathered several children. The family became affluent, for John's extensive land holdings included a 5,000-acre tract on the Potomac River, including what later became the Mount Vernon estate, the home of George Washington.

John's younger brother, Lawrence, benefited most from Andrew Knowling's will, and inherited lands forming part of the Manor of Great Tring. In the early months of 1659 Lawrence paid a visit to his brother in Virginia, and decided to join him there. Before he finally settled, he returned to England to marry in Luton, and to visit Tring to raise money from his property at Frogmore End and other land. This is believed to have financed his trading ventures in Virginia, where he died in 1677.

Martha was the third of Amphyllis's children to emigrate from Tring to Virginia. In his will her brother, John, left £10 for her passage to the new colony, and arranged accommodation for her on arrival. When Martha died she left a small bequest to John's grandson, Augustine. This man was the father of George Washington who became the first president of the United States, and esteemed by generations of Americans as "first in war, first in peace, and first in the hearts of his countrymen".

Sources

New England Historical and Genealogical Register, Peter Walne, 1975

Hertfordshire Countryside, Peter Walne, July 1975

Hertfordshire Countryside, Dr Doris Jones-Baker, September 1979

Tring Parish Magazines, 1918 and 1919

The alternative name of the Glis Glis is the Fat or Edible Dormouse, and this is no surprise when we learn that it was considered a scrumptious snack by the Romans, who kept them in special enclosures (called gliraria). As they grew they were removed to earthenware jars, and fattened on honey.

Two thousand years later, a small number of these little creatures encountered better fortune when a few were liberated in Tring Park. Whether by design or accident is not known, but the culprit was certainly Walter Rothschild who had brought to Tring some of Europe's largest dormice to keep as pets. It was soon rumoured that they were damaging crops, as well as thatched roofs, and immediate steps were taken to trap them. In spite of vigorous efforts, some remained at large, and one hundred years later descendents of the Tring Glis Glis now roam over six counties. The Glis Glis holds the distinction of being the only species of mammal that is solely from Hertfordshire and has been successfully introduced to Britain, but it is a pity that it cannot be viewed as a welcome addition to the country's wild life.

Some say the origin of its name derives from the unforgettable call, which can be imitated by repeatedly saying 'glis glis glis' in a deep voice with a fixed grin and heavy lisp. More likely the source is the Latin word 'glinis' - a dormouse.

There are several reasons for this furry little animal's deep unpopularity. The Glis Glis has the misfortune to resemble closely a notorious countryside pest - the grey squirrel. He is smaller, but has a similar flat rudder-like tail and fur coloration which differs only in having a little brown on the back, and dark rings round the eyes.

Glis Glis (Edible Dormouse)

At first glance his feeding habits look harmless, as nuts and fruits comprise a great part of his diet. But when those fruits happen to be apples, the troubles start for human kind. Apples may be stored in sheds or lofts of houses, and the Glis Glis is an agile climber and can make enormous leaps. Having acquired a taste for loft-living, and a widening of his diet to include insulation round electric wiring, the Glis Glis will happily indulge his noctural habits by scurrying round an attic in the small hours. It is said that his four tiny feet can sound like a miniature rugby scrum.

When autumn comes, all is silence, and people may breathe a sigh of relief and think that their uninvited guest has departed. After seven months most will have forgotten the irritation of the previous year, but come the next spring a familar pattering overhead tells them that the Glis Glis has returned. In fact he has never been away, merely enjoying the deep sleep of hibernation, possibly cosily ensconced inside a roll of spare carpet or in grandma's old fur coat. Understandably, members of afflicted households may attempt to trap him, but no one takes pleasure in killing such an appealing-looking creature, and very often he is taken some distance away to be released into the wild, although this increases the spread of his species.

Once back outside, the Glis Glis fashions a neat nest lined with moss and grasses, his favourite sites being in low trees, in holes in walls, or in fact anywhere near the ground. At the end of the summer, when his family of up to eight young are safely reared, they will leave the nest to seek out pastures (or lofts) new.

Sources

Hertfordshire Countryside, February 1971
Mammals, Amphibians and Reptiles of Hertfordshire, Michael Clark 2001
Natural History of Britain & Europe, Michael Chinery 1992